THE CLASSROOM ORGANIZER

201 Ready-to-Use Forms for K–8 Teachers and Administrators

Antonia Ballare & Angelique Lampros

PARKER PUBLISHING COMPANY
West Nyack, New York 10995

ISBN 0-13-136870-2

PARKER PUBLISHING COMPANY
BUSINESS & PROFESSIONAL DIVISION
A division of Simon & Schuster
West Nyack, New York 10995

Dedication

We dedicate this book to each other,
without whose warm friendship, mutual respect,
common philosophy and steadfast resolve it
probably would not have been written.

Acknowledgments

We recognize and appreciate the support
of our families and colleagues, Rocco Tomazic's
expertise, and Evelyn Fazio's encouragement.

About the Authors

Antonia Ballare earned her B.S. from Trenton State College in New Jersey, her M.Ed. in Elementary Reading from Boston University, and has continued taking graduate courses in elementary education. Currently a third-grade teacher at Seth Boyden School in Maplewood, New Jersey, she has served as co-chairperson of the Reorganization of the Elementary School Day Task Force and as a chairperson of the Professional Rights and Responsibilities Committee of the South Orange-Maplewood Education Association.

Angelique Lampros earned her B.A. in Secondary Science Education from Montclair State College in New Jersey, her M.A. in Elementary Administration from George Washington University, and has taken additional graduate courses at Seton Hall University, Kean College, and Fordham University. Currently a basic skills improvement/resource teacher at Seth Boyden School in Maplewood, New Jersey, she has taught at both elementary and secondary levels and has been an acting principal. Ms. Lampros has served as chairperson of the Middle States Association Community Self-Study, co-chairperson of the Reorganization of the Elementary School Day Task Force for the district of South Orange-Maplewood, and authored a national public relations guide for the Citizens' Reading Council in Washington, D.C.

The authors have been friends and colleagues for over twenty years. They first met while teaching at Jefferson School in the district of South Orange-Maplewood, New Jersey. Similar philosophies of education led them to collaborate in team-teaching, the development of classroom management techniques, and a staff development workshop for the district on the subject.

About This Book

The Classroom Organizer: 201 Ready-to-Use Forms for K–8 Teachers and Administrators is designed to help you take immediate control of every facet of classroom management and organization. School district standards are achieved when administrators and teachers work together, so both groups will find that this book's more than 200 reproducible forms will help maximize school time for themselves, their students, and parents.

All forms are numbered for easy location, and several sample pages are also included to offer models for creating new forms. Each section's brief introduction is followed by specific notes that help clarify the usefulness of particular forms. The forms cover a wide range of objectives which will help you:

- Inventory materials
- Arrange facilities
- Maintain collections/equipment
- Share information
- Schedule subjects/activities
- Simplify planning
- Record personal/academic history
- Evaluate progress
- Foster work habits/study skills
- Clarify assignments
- Individualize learning
- Foster responsibility
- Encourage self-evaluation
- Clarify thinking
- Reward growth/progress
- Celebrate accomplishments
- Promote self-discipline
- Reinforce concepts
- Schedule parent conferences
- Inform parents
- Invite parent input
- Maximize field trips
- Encourage professional growth

The Classroom Organizer is divided into the following four major sections:

- Section I, ORGANIZATIONAL FORMS FOR THE CLASSROOM, helps to organize facilities and materials, simplify planning and teaching, systematize evaluating and record keeping, and maintain communication with colleagues. The 75 forms found in this section include "Classroom Equipment Inventory," "Bulletin Board Form," "Classroom Seating Chart," "Substitute Teacher's Procedures Form," "Computer Record Keeping," "Creative Writing Evaluation," "Discipline Record," and "Bill/Receipt for Lost Material."

- Section II, FORMS TO USE WITH STUDENTS, has forms to structure curriculum, organize student time and materials, and foster personal growth and development. The 62 forms offered in this section include "Multi-Assignment Reminder," "My At-Home Reading Calendar," "Absentee's Homework Assignment Sheet," "Individualized Planning Chart," "Classroom Rules Form for Students," and "Success Certificate."

- Section III, FORMS FOR COMMUNICATING WITH PARENTS, helps to inform parents of any classroom's comprehensive program throughout the year, report student progress, and invite parent participation as resources and volunteers. The 55 forms in this section include "Parent's Personal Data Request Form," "Conference Letter," "Specialist's Evaluation for Parents," "Behavior Report," "Parent Volunteer Record," and "Field Trip Instruction Packet."

- Section IV, FORMS FOR PROFESSIONAL GROWTH AND DEVELOPMENT, helps teachers to achieve work-related goals in the classroom by means of self-evaluation. Other forms assist teachers in maintaining, developing, and improving their professional expertise. The 10 forms in this section include "Convention/Conference Expense Record," "Resume Planning Form," and "Self-Evaluation for the Teacher/Manager."

It is not enough to impart knowledge through well-planned lessons, nor to know how or to what degree students learn. Education is most effective when firmly supported by understanding and by applying classroom dynamics, that is, managing and organizing every aspect of classroom activity. Recognizing the difficulty in being held accountable for an efficiently run classroom while still having time and energy for creative planning and teaching, this book lightens the frustrating burden of "getting organized." *The Classroom Organizer: 201 Ready-to-Use Forms for K–8 Teachers and Administrators* delivers what its title promises and, along with it, professional peace of mind!

Antonia Ballare
Angelique Lampros

Contents

Section II
FORMS TO USE WITH STUDENTS • 85

Section III
FORMS FOR COMMUNICATING WITH PARENTS • 155

Section IV
FORMS FOR PROFESSIONAL GROWTH AND DEVELOPMENT • 221

ORGANIZATIONAL FORMS FOR THE CLASSROOM

Organized classroom facilities and materials and preset classroom procedures get the school year off to a favorable start. Structure expedites planning and directs sequential skill development. Thorough evaluation guides teaching. The educational process is enhanced as colleagues support each other through effective communication concerning their students.

EXPLANATORY NOTES

Form IA–8: In the third column, "type of material" can refer to text, a kit, a game, a manipulative, filmstrips, and so on.

Form IB–10: Make horizontal lines to suit your needs.

Form IB–11: After listing pullouts for each of Monday's subjects, extend the next line to the left for Tuesday and so forth. (See note for IB–19.)

Form IB–19: Insert this along with the "Substitute Teacher's Procedures Form,""Pull-Out Schedule," and your own instructional materials for an almost foolproof sick day.

Form IB–20: See note for IB–19.

Form IC–1: Question 1 assesses "Independence"; questions 2–3, "Organization"; questions 4–5, "Cooperation"; question 6, "Self-Image"; questions 7–9, "Responsibility"; questions 10–11, "Attitude and Concentration"; and question 12, "Respect."

Form ID–7: This form can facilitate the scheduling of consecutive conferences for parents who have more than one child in the same school.

Organizing Facilities and Materials

List	Have	Need	List	Have	Need
1. Class List			31. *Books:*		
2. Attendance Forms			Classroom Library		
3. Paper			Reading		
4. Pencils			Math		
5. Pens			Social Studies		
6. Erasers			Science		
7. Chalk			Health		
8. Chalkboard Erasers			English		
9. Crayons			Dictionaries		
10. Construction Paper			_____		
11. Ditto Masters			_____		
12. Copier Paper			_____		
13. Masking Tape			32. Kits		
14. Seating Charts			33. Fire Exit Sign		
15. Pencil Sharpener			34. Desk Supplies		
16. Requisition Forms			35. Rulers		
17. First Day Procedures			36. Yardstick		
18. Flag			37. Placement Tests		
19. Lesson Plans			38. Diagnostic Tests		
20. Student Records			39. Wall Maps		
21. School Procedures			40. Globe		
22. Schedule of Specialists			41. Student Desk/Chairs		
23. Schedule of Nurse			42. Work Tables		
24. Schedule of Librarian			43. Teacher's Desk/Chair		
25. Schedule Support Staff			44. Bookcases/Shelves		
26. Schedule of Assemblies			45. Filing Cabinet(s)		
27. Weekly Schedule			46. Keys for Room, Cabinets		
28. List of Staff			47. Stapler/Remover		
29. Teacher's Manuals			48. Scissors		
30. Curriculum Guides			49. Hole Puncher		

Supply	On Hand	Order	Supply	On Hand	Order
1. *Art Supplies:*			16. Bookends		
Construction Paper			17. Lesson Plan Book		
Paint			18. Attendance Book		
Brushes			19. Grade Book		
Felt Markers			20. Copier Paper		
Cardboard			21. White Out		
Crayons			22. Envelopes		
Cray-pas			23. Chalk		
Oaktag			24. *Rulers:*		
Mural Paper			Inches		
Paste			Yardstick(s)		
Glue			Metric		
Duco-cement			25. Protractors		
String			26. Compasses		
Colored Yarn			27. *File Folders:*		
Metallic Paper			Letter		
Tissue Paper			Legal		
Glitter			28. Pocket Folders		
2. Paper Clips			29. Composition Books		
3. Rubber Bands			30. Note Books		
4. Stapler(s)			31. Pencils		
5. Staples			32. Erasers		
6. Staple Remover			33. Masking Tape		
7. Thumb Tacks			34. Transparent Tape		
8. Brass Fasteners			35. *Paper:*		
9. Hole Puncher			_____		
10. *Scissors:*			_____		
Student			_____		
Teacher			_____		
11. Safety Pins			36. Pens		
12. Straight Pins			37. Grease Pencils		
13. Labels			38. Magic Markers		
14. Index Cards			39. Tissues		
15. Reinforcements			40. _____		

Audio-Visual Equipment	Computers
Wall Maps and Globes	**Games**
Kits	
	Miscellany

IA–4

TEACHER'S MANUAL AND REFERENCE BOOK INVENTORY

Subject	Title	Level	Publisher

TEXTBOOK INVENTORY

Subject	Title	Level	Quantity	Publisher

IA–5

AUDIO-VISUAL REORDER FORM

Key:

P:	(Pictures)	MP:	(8mm)
VC:	(Video-cassette)	VT:	(Videotape)
S:	(Slides)	C:	(Computer software)
T:	(Transparencies)	R:	(Record)
FS:	(Filmstrip)	TP:	(Tape)

Subject	Unit	Title	Description	Type of A-V	Color

INVENTORY AND REORDERING FORM

			FALL			SPRING		
ITEM	VENDOR	CATALOG NUMBER	QUANTITY	PRICE	TOTAL COST	QUANTITY	PRICE	TOTAL COST

IA–8   YEAR-END TEACHING MATERIALS PURCHASE ORDER REQUEST

TEACHER: _____   DATE: _____

VENDOR	TITLE OR NAME OF MATERIAL	TYPE OF MATERIAL	CATALOG NUMBER	PAGE	PRICE PER UNIT	QUANTITY

MATERIALS REQUEST FORM

To: _____ Date: _____

From: _____

Please get me the following materials:

_____
_____
_____
_____
_____
_____
_____
_____
_____
_____

MATERIALS REQUEST FORM

To: _____ Date: _____

From: _____

Please get me the following materials:

_____
_____
_____
_____
_____
_____
_____
_____
_____

TEACHER'S FORM FOR BORROWING TEXTS   IA–10

To: _____   Date: _____

From: _____   Grade: _____

Re: _____
    Subject(s)

Need: _____ _____ _____
       Number   Title   Grade Level

       _____ _____ _____
       Number   Title   Grade Level

       _____ _____ _____
       Number   Title   Grade Level

       _____ _____ _____
       Number   Title   Grade Level

       _____ _____ _____
       Number   Title   Grade Level

       _____ _____ _____
       Number   Title   Grade Level

TEACHER'S FORM FOR BORROWING TEXTS

To: _____   Date: _____

From: _____   Grade: _____

Re: _____
    Subject(s)

Need: _____ _____ _____
       Number   Title   Grade Level

       _____ _____ _____
       Number   Title   Grade Level

       _____ _____ _____
       Number   Title   Grade Level

       _____ _____ _____
       Number   Title   Grade Level

       _____ _____ _____
       Number   Title   Grade Level

       _____ _____ _____
       Number   Title   Grade Level

IA–11   TEACHER'S FORM FOR RETURN OF TEXTS AND MATERIALS

To: _____   Date: _____

From: _____

Re: *The following materials are being returned:*

_____   _____
Subject   _____

                               _____

                               _____

_____   _____
Subject   _____

                               _____

                               _____

_____   _____
Subject   _____

                               _____

                               _____

_____   _____
Subject   _____

                               _____

                               _____

_____   _____
Other   _____

                               _____

                               _____

14

Student	Material Borrowed	Date Borrowed	Date Returned

BULLETIN BOARD FORM

TEACHER: _____   YEAR: _____

Idea/Subject	Date	Materials Used	Color Scheme	Work Teacher/Student

Section IB

Planning
and
Instruction

SUBJECT: _____

	Item or Objective																		
Name	**Date**																		
1. _____																			
2. _____																			
3. _____																			
4. _____																			
5. _____																			
6. _____																			
7. _____																			
8. _____																			
9. _____																			
10. _____																			
11. _____																			
12. _____																			
13. _____																			
14. _____																			
15. _____																			
16. _____																			
17. _____																			
18. _____																			
19. _____																			
20. _____																			
21. _____																			
22. _____																			
23. _____																			
24. _____																			
25. _____																			
26. _____																			
27. _____																			

IB–3   CLASS LIST—DIAGNOSTIC/ACADEMIC—READING

TEACHER: _____   GRADE: _____   YEAR: _____

| Students | Standardized Test ( ) Level ( ) Total Reading | | | Reading Placement Test ( ) | | |
	Pretest-Yr. ( )	Post-Test-Yr. ( )	Growth	Pretest	Post-Test	Growth
1)						
2)						
3)						
4)						
5)						
6)						
7)						
8)						
9)						
10)						
11)						
12)						
13)						
14)						
15)						
16)						
17)						
18)						
19)						
20)						
21)						
22)						
23)						
24)						
25)						
26)						
27)						

IB–4

CLASS LIST—DIAGNOSTIC/ACADEMIC—MATH

TEACHER: _____ GRADE: _____ YEAR _____

Students	Standardized Test ( ) Level ( ) Total Math			Math Placement Test ( )		
	Pretest-Yr. ( )	Post-Test-Yr. ( )	Growth	Pretest	Post-Test	Growth
1)						
2)						
3)						
4)						
5)						
6)						
7)						
8)						
9)						
10)						
11)						
12)						
13)						
14)						
15)						
16)						
17)						
18)						
19)						
20)						
21)						
22)						
23)						
24)						
25)						
26)						
27)						

IB–5 CLASS LIST—DIAGNOSTIC/ACADEMIC—LANGUAGE/WRITING

TEACHER: _____ GRADE: _____ YEAR: _____

Students	Standardized Test ( ) Level ( ) Total Language			Writing Sample (Holistic)		
	Pretest-Yr. ( )	Post-Test-Yr. ( )	Growth	Pretest	Post-Test	Growth
1)						
2)						
3)						
4)						
5)						
6)						
7)						
8)						
9)						
10)						
11)						
12)						
13)						
14)						
15)						
16)						
17)						
18)						
19)						
20)						
21)						
22)						
23)						
24)						
25)						
26)						
27)						

IB–6   CLASS LIST—DIAGNOSTIC/ACADEMIC—LANGUAGE/SPELLING

TEACHER: _____   GRADE: _____   YEAR: _____

| Students | Standardized Test ( ) Level ( ) Spelling | | | Spelling Placement Test ( ) | | |
	Pretest-Yr. ( )	Post-Test-Yr. ( )	Growth	Pretest	Post-Test	Growth
1)						
2)						
3)						
4)						
5)						
6)						
7)						
8)						
9)						
10)						
11)						
12)						
13)						
14)						
15)						
16)						
17)						
18)						
19)						
20)						
21)						
22)						
23)						
24)						
25)						
26)						
27)						

IB–7

CURRICULUM MAPPING FORM

SUBJECT: _____

Dates	Objectives	Materials Used to Teach

Schedule for Grade: _____

TEACHER: _____   GRADE: _____   YEAR: _____

Time	Monday	Tuesday	Wednesday	Thursday	Friday

WEEKLY SCHEDULE (SAMPLE)

TEACHER: _____   GRADE: _____   YEAR: _____

	MONDAY	TUESDAY	WEDNESDAY	THURSDAY	FRIDAY
8:30–8:40	←———————— ATTENDANCE—OPENING EXERCISES ————————→				
8:40–9:00	SPELLING	SPELLING	SPELLING	SPELLING	SPELLING
9:00–9:30	ORAL AND WRITTEN LANGUAGE	ORAL AND WRITTEN LANGUAGE	HANDWRITING	ORAL AND WRITTEN LANGUAGE	HANDWRITING
9:30–10:20	ART	MATH	PHYSICAL EDUCATION	MUSIC	MATH
10:30	WORK PERIOD		WORK PERIOD	WORK PERIOD	
10:30–11:30	READING	READING	READING	READING	READING
11:30–12:30	LUNCH	LUNCH	LUNCH	LUNCH	LUNCH
12:30–12:40	MATH	ORGANIZATION TIME			
1:30 / 1:40		12:40–1:40 SCIENCE AND SOCIAL STUDIES (½ hr. each)	MATH	MATH	12:40–1:10 IND. WORK PERIOD
2:00	HEALTH AND SAFETY	1:45–2:20 PHYS. EDUC.	1:45–2:45 SCIENCE AND SOC. STU. (½ hr. each)	1:45–2:45 SCIENCE AND SOC. STU. (½ hr. each)	1:10–1:45 PHYS. EDUC.
	ORAL AND WRITTEN LANGUAGE	2:20–3:00 ORAL AND WRITTEN LANGUAGE			
	2:40–2:55 SILENT READING		2:45–3:00 ←—CURRENT EVENTS—→		2:50–3:00 CLEAN-UP
3:00	CLEAN-UP				
3:10	←————————— DISMISSAL ————————————→				

IB–10

SPECIALIST'S SCHEDULE FORM

TIME	MONDAY	TUESDAY	WEDNESDAY	THURSDAY	FRIDAY

Day	Student	Subject	Time

IB–12

MONTHLY PLANING CALENDAR

TEACHER: _____

GRADE: _____

YEAR: _____

   I.   Objective(s) of lesson:

  II.   Motivation:

 III.   Development of lesson:
            [Includes demonstration model, feedback, practice exercises.]

 IV.   Evaluation of student learning:

  V.   Self-evaluation:
            [Did you achieve the objective? What else could have been done (alternative ways)? Were there any problems (what were they)? What will be the following?]

TEACHER: _____ GRADE: _____

Day: Date:	Special Events
	Dittos to Prepare
	Dittos to Run Off
	Future Plans
Comments	

IB–15   WEEKLY LESSON PLAN FORM—SINGLE SUBJECT

TEACHER: _____   SUBJECT: _____

GRADE OR ROOM: _____   WEEK OF: _____

Monday

Tuesday

Wednesday

Thursday

Friday

TEACHER: Mrs. Jones   **GRADE:** Four

DATE: Monday, October 4th   **ROOM:** 10

Time	SUBJECT AND PLANS	
8:30–8:40	ATTENDANCE: LUNCH BOX: LUNCH PROGRAM SLIP: OPENING EXERCISES:	
8:40–9:30	ORAL AND WRITTEN LANGUAGE:	
9:30–10:20	MUSIC (with Mrs. Russo):	
10:20–10:25	ACTIVITY PERIOD:	
10:25–11:30	READING GROUP:	READING GROUP:
11:30–12:30	LUNCH:	
12:30–1:30	MATH GROUP:	MATH GROUP:
1:30–2:20	ART (with Mr. Mitchell):	
2:20–2:50	HEALTH AND SAFETY:	
2:50–3:00	ACTIVITY PERIOD: Do class jobs and prepare for dismissal.	
3:00	DISMISSAL:	

DAY: _____   DATE: _____

CALL   MEET

MAKE   WRITE

COPY   FILE

CORRECT   PICK-UP

ORDER   OTHER

DAY: _____   DATE: _____

CALL   MEET

MAKE   WRITE

COPY   FILE

CORRECT   PICK-UP

ORDER   OTHER

DAY: _____   DATE: _____

CALL   MEET

MAKE   WRITE

COPY   FILE

CORRECT   PICK-UP

ORDER   OTHER

DAY: _____   DATE: _____

CALL   MEET

MAKE   WRITE

COPY   FILE

CORRECT   PICK-UP

ORDER   OTHER

DAY: _____   DATE: _____

CALL   MEET

MAKE   WRITE

COPY   FILE

CORRECT   PICK-UP

ORDER   OTHER

TEAM-TEACHING PLANNING FORM IB–18

Teacher: _____ Grade: _____

Teammate: _____ Grade: _____

Subjects Teaming in: _____

Days Teaming: _____
_____

Time Teaming: _____

Objectives for Each Subject: _____
_____
_____
_____
_____
_____
_____
_____
_____
_____
_____
_____
_____

Additional Comments: _____
_____
_____
_____
_____
_____
_____
_____
_____
_____
_____
_____
_____
_____

EMERGENCY LESSON PLAN

Teacher: _____   Grade: _____

#1
Subject: _____	Materials: _____

Things to Know: _____

Things to Do: _____

_____

#2
Subject: _____	Materials: _____

Things to Know: _____

Things to Do: _____

_____

#3
Subject: _____	Materials: _____

Things to Know: _____

Things to Do: _____

_____

#4
Subject: _____	Materials: _____

Things to Know: _____

Things to Do: _____

_____

SUBSTITUTE TEACHER'S PROCEDURES   IB–20

This form has been carefully completed by the regular classroom teacher, _____,
so that your day can be as efficient, productive and pleasant as possible. Please read and use
the information below.

School: _____   Principal: _____

Grade: _____   Room Number: _____   School year: _____

Morning Session: _____ - _____   Afternoon Session: _____ - _____

Entering Procedure _____

_____

_____

Dismissal Procedure _____

_____

_____

Lunch Period: _____ - _____

Lunch Money Collection Procedure _____

_____

_____

Lunch Procedure _____

_____

_____

- -

Location of Daily Plan _____

Location of Emergency Plan _____

Location of Weekly Schedule _____

Location of Seating Chart(s) _____

- -

Attendance Procedure _____

_____

Lavatory Procedure _____

_____

Hall Pass Procedure _____

_____

Fire Drill Procedure _____

_____

Library Media Center Procedure _____

_____

Student Locker Procedure _____

_____

Student Illness Procedure _____

_____

_____

- -

Students with Medical Problems: (Seek aid immediately)

Student: _____   Problem: _____

Student: _____   Problem: _____

Student: _____   Problem: _____

Student: _____   Problem: _____

Student: _____   Problem: _____

Student Leaders:

_____   _____

_____   _____

Behavior Problems:

Student: _____   Helpful Info.: _____

Student: _____   Helpful Info.: _____

Student: _____   Helpful Info.: _____

Student: _____   Helpful Info.: _____

Student: _____   Helpful Info.: _____

Student: _____   Helpful Info.: _____

Student: _____   Helpful Info.: _____

School Disciplinary Procedure:

_____

_____

_____

STUDENT TEACHER: _____   COOPERATING TEACHER: _____

WEEK NUMBER: _____ OF PRACTICUM   WEEK OF: _____

Day	Observe	Teach	Assist
M O N D A Y			
T U E S D A Y			
W E D N E S D A Y			
T H U R S D A Y			
F R I D A Y			

IB–22 STUDENT SIGN-OUT SHEET FOR OUT-OF-CLASS ACTIVITIES

STUDENT: PLEASE SIGN YOUR NAME, WHERE YOU ARE GOING AND THE TIME YOU ARE LEAVING THIS CLASSROOM. THANK YOU.

Day	Name	Where Going (Teacher or Place)	Time

© 1989 by Parker Publishing Company

IB–23

SHARING-TIME CALENDAR FOR STUDENT ACTIVITIES

PLEASE SIGN YOUR NAME(S) UNDER THE DATE YOU WISH TO MAKE YOUR PRESENTATION.

	MONDAY	TUESDAY	WEDNESDAY	THURSDAY	FRIDAY
Week of					
Week of					
Week of					
Week of					

IB–24 ASSIGNMENT/ACTIVITY RECORD—INDIVIDUAL

STUDENT'S NAME: _____   SUBJECT(S): _____

Date Given	Assignment or Activity	Date Due	Received	Late

NAME OF GROUP: _____   SUBJECT(S): _____

Students in Group

_____   _____   _____

_____   _____   _____

_____   _____   _____

Date Given	Assignment or Activity

IB–26   # SAFETY PATROL CANDIDATES FORM

To: _____
(Classroom Teacher/s)

From: _____
(Safety Patrol Advisor/s)

Date: _____ in preparation for the _____ – _____ school year.

Please submit a list of possible candidates from your classroom who are dependable and interested in serving next year on the Safety Patrol by _____.
(Date)

- -

Teacher: _____   Grade: _____

Name of Student   **Name of Student**

1. _____   11. _____
2. _____   12. _____
3. _____   13. _____
4. _____   14. _____
5. _____   15. _____
6. _____   16. _____
7. _____   17. _____
8. _____   18. _____
9. _____   19. _____
10. _____   20. _____

IB–27

SAFETY PATROL POST ASSIGNMENT RECORD

YEAR: _____

MONTH: _____

Student	Teacher	Telephone Number	Substitute	Teacher	Telephone Number	Assigned Street(s)

IB-28

SAFETY PATROL EQUIPMENT RECORD

YEAR: _____ MONTH: _____

Student	Raingear		Belt		Badge	
		Number		Number		Number
1.						
2.						
3.						
4.						
5.						
6.						
7.						
8.						
9.						
10.						
11.						
12.						
13.						
14.						
15.						
16.						
17.						
18.						
19.						
20.						
21.						
22.						
23.						
24.						
25.						
26.						
27.						

Please have elections for _____ representatives and _____
　　　　　　　　　　　　　　　(Number)　　　　　　　　　　　　　　　　　(Number)

alternates from your class the week of _____.
　　　　　　　　　　　　　　　　　　　　　　　　(Date)

Enclosed is a copy of the _____ constitution
　　　　　　　　　　　　　　　　　(Name of School)

to review with your class before nominations and elections.

Please stress competency of students elected rather than popularity.

_____ Representatives:_____
(Number)

　　　　　　　　_____

　　　　　　　　_____

_____ Alternates:　　_____
(Number)

　　　　　　　　　　　　_____

　　　　　　　　　　　　_____

Teacher: _____   Grade: _____

Please send to me by _____.
　　　　　　　　　　　　　(Date)

Thank You!

_____
Student Council Advisor

STUDENT COUNCIL ANNOUNCEMENT

_____   _____
(Project/s)   (Month/s)

The Student Council is requesting that each class discuss and vote whether or not to proceed with plans to implement the above project/s for the school year _____.

Please discuss alternatives and return ballot results to

_____ by _____.
(Student Council Advisor)   (Date)

Teacher's Name: _____   Number of Students
                                             Who Voted _____

Alternative Suggestions: _____

_____

_____

_____

_____

- -

STUDENT COUNCIL ANNOUNCEMENT FORM

_____   _____
(Project/s)   (Month/s)

The Student Council is requesting that each class discuss and vote whether or not to proceed with plans to implement the above project/s for the school year _____.

Please discuss alternatives and return ballot results to

_____ by _____.
(Student Council Advisor)   (Date)

Teacher's Name: _____   Number of Students
                                             Who Voted _____

Alternative Suggestions: _____

_____

_____

_____

_____
(Date)

_____
(Time)

_____
(Place)

AGENDA

I.   CALL TO ORDER

II. MINUTES OF PREVIOUS MEETING

III. TREASURER'S REPORT

IV. COMMITTEE REPORTS

_____
_____
_____
_____
_____
_____
_____
_____
_____
_____
_____

V. NEW BUSINESS

_____
_____
_____
_____
_____
_____
_____
_____
_____
_____
_____
_____
_____
_____

IB–32 STUDENT COUNCIL ACTIVITIES/FUND RAISING
School Year _____–_____

School
Project: _____

Date to be
Completed: _____

   Needs:

   1. _____

   2. _____

   3. _____

   4. _____

   5. _____

School
Project: _____

Date to be
Completed: _____

   Needs:

   1. _____

   2. _____

   3. _____

   4. _____

   5. _____

School
Project: _____

Date to be
Completed: _____

   Needs:

   1. _____

   2. _____

   3. _____

   4. _____

   5. _____

_____   _____   _____
Student Council President   Student Council Advisor   Principal

Meeting called to order by _____
(President)

at _____. Minutes of previous meeting read
(Day, Time)

by _____. Minutes approved as
(Secretary)

_____. Treasurer's report read by
(Read or Corrected)

_____ and approved as
(Treasurer)

_____.
(Read or Corrected)

_____

_____

_____

_____

_____

_____

_____

_____

_____

_____

_____

_____

_____

_____

_____

_____

_____

_____ made a motion to adjourn the meeting at
(Representative)

_____. Seconded by _____.
(Time)   (Representative)

Respectfully Submitted,

_____
(Secretary's Name)

STUDENT COUNCIL TREASURER'S MONTHLY FORM

PROJECT(S): _____   MONTH: _____

INCOME

EXPENSES

_____
Total Monthly Income

_____
Total Monthly Expenses

_____
Balance

_____
Date of Report

_____
Treasurer's Signature

© 1989 by Parker Publishing Company

- -

STUDENT COUNCIL TREASURER'S MONTHLY FORM

PROJECT(S): _____   MONTH: _____

INCOME

EXPENSES

_____
Total Monthly Income

_____
Total Monthly Expenses

_____
Balance

_____
Date of Report

_____
Treasurer's Signature

STUDENT COUNCIL TREASURER'S ANNUAL FORM   IB–35

Project	Income	Expenses	Balance
Project	Income	Expenses	Balance
Project	Income	Expenses	Balance
Project	Income	Expenses	Balance
Project	Income	Expenses	Balance
Project	Income	Expenses	Balance
Project	Income	Expenses	Balance
Project	Income	Expenses	Balance
Project	Income	Expenses	Balance
Project	Income	Expenses	Balance
	Total Income	Total Expenses	Final Balance

Year

Treasurer's Signature

Advisor's Signature

Principal's Signature

Keeping
Records
and
Evaluation

AFFECTIVE ASSESSMENT

NAME: _____ GRADE: _____

TEACHER: _____

Key to Checklist: C-Consistently I-Inconsistently S-Seldom	Fall			Spring		
	C	I	S	C	I	S
1. Completes assignments on his/her own.						
2. Organizes materials and time effectively.						
3. Submits neat, well-planned assignments.						
4. Participates in teacher-directed activities.						
5. Interacts well with peers.						
6. Accepts classroom and school rules and consequences.						
7. Takes pride in personal appearance and accomplishments.						
8. Begins and completes assignments on time.						
9. Behaves well in class.						
10. Regards attendance and promptness as important.						
11. Is an interested, conscientious student.						
12. Follows oral and written directions and accepts constructive criticism.						
13. Shows concern for others and for school property.						

IC–2

PLACEMENT DATA FOR BASIC SKILLS GROUPING

TEACHER: _____ GRADE: _____ YEAR: _____

Student's Name	READING						MATH					
	Standardized Test/Score	Level	Date	Placement Test/Score	Level	Date	Standardized Test/Score	Level	Date	Placement Test/Score	Level	Date
1.												
2.												
3.												
4.												
5.												
6.												
7.												
8.												
9.												
10.												
11.												
12.												
13.												
14.												
15.												
16.												
17.												
18.												
19.												
20.												
21.												
22.												
23.												
24.												
25.												
26.												
27.												

IC–3

INDIVIDUAL LONG-TERM STANDARDIZED TEST RECORD

STUDENT'S NAME: _____

TEST NAME: _____

Subject	Grade	Year	National Percentile	Grade	Year	National Percentile	Grade	Year	National Percentile	Grade	Year	National Percentile
Reading												
Word Attack												
Vocabulary												
Comprehension												
Total Reading												
Spelling												
Language												
Mechanics												
Expression												
Total Language												
Mathematics												
Computation												
Concepts/Application												
Total Mathematics												
Total Battery												

COMMENTS:

SUBJECT: _____

Student's Name	Date:										
1.											
2.											
3.											
4.											
5.											
6.											
7.											
8.											
9.											
10.											
11.											
12.											
13.											
14.											
Pages											
Objective											

NAME: _____   CLASS: _____

Grade	Objective	Lesson Number	Date Assigned	Date Completed	Score	Next Assignment

TEACHER: _____ GRADE: _____

OBJECTIVE: _____

Student Name	Lesson Number	Date Assigned	Date Completed	Comments

PERSONAL DEVELOPMENT EVALUATION

TEACHER: _____

Student	FALL						WINTER						SPRING					
	SELF CONTROL	POLITE	CONSIDERATE	COOPERATIVE	POSITIVE	ATTITUDE	SELF CONTROL	POLITE	CONSIDERATE	COOPERATIVE	POSITIVE	ATTITUDE	SELF CONTROL	POLITE	CONSIDERATE	COOPERATIVE	POSITIVE	ATTITUDE
1. _____																		
2. _____																		
3. _____																		
4. _____																		
5. _____																		
6. _____																		
7. _____																		
8. _____																		
9. _____																		
10. _____																		
11. _____																		
12. _____																		
13. _____																		
14. _____																		
15. _____																		
16. _____																		
17. _____																		
18. _____																		
19. _____																		
20. _____																		
21. _____																		
22. _____																		
23. _____																		
24. _____																		
25. _____																		
26. _____																		
27. _____																		

INDIVIDUAL EVALUATION OF READING—PRIMARY IC–8

GROUP: _____   STUDENT: _____

TITLE:
WORD ANALYSIS:
VOCABULARY:
COMPREHENSION:
ORAL READING:
COMMENT:

TITLE:
WORD ANALYSIS:
VOCABULARY:
COMPREHENSION:
ORAL READING:
COMMENT:

TITLE:
WORD ANALYSIS:
VOCABULARY:
COMPREHENSION:
ORAL READING:
COMMENT:

TITLE:
WORD ANALYSIS:
VOCABULARY:
COMPREHENSION:
ORAL READING:
COMMENT:

TITLE:
WORD ANALYSIS:
VOCABULARY:
COMPREHENSION:
ORAL READING:
COMMENT:

TITLE:
WORD ANALYSIS:
VOCABULARY:
COMPREHENSION:
ORAL READING:
COMMENT:

GROUP: _____   STUDENT: _____

TITLE:
WORD ANALYSIS:
VOCABULARY:
COMPREHENSION:
Literal:
Interpretive:
Evaluative:
Creative:
ORAL READING:
COMMENT:

TITLE:
WORD ANALYSIS:
VOCABULARY:
COMPREHENSION:
Literal:
Interpretive:
Evaluative:
Creative:
ORAL READING:
COMMENT:

TITLE:
WORD ANALYSIS:
VOCABULARY:
COMPREHENSION:
Literal:
Interpretive:
Evaluative:
Creative:
ORAL READING:
COMMENT:

TITLE:
WORD ANALYSIS:
VOCABULARY:
COMPREHENSION:
Literal:
Interpretive:
Evaluative:
Creative:
ORAL READING:
COMMENT:

TITLE:
WORD ANALYSIS:
VOCABULARY:
COMPREHENSION:
Literal:
Interpretive:
Evaluative:
Creative:
ORAL READING:
COMMENT:

TITLE:
WORD ANALYSIS:
VOCABULARY:
COMPREHENSION:
Literal:
Interpretive:
Evaluative:
Creative:
ORAL READING:
COMMENT:

CREATIVE WRITING EVALUATION

NAME: _____

DATE (OR YEAR): _____ GRADE: _____ ROOM: _____

	Did Well!	Try To Improve		Did Well!	Try To Imrpve
Assignment(s) completed on time					
FORMAT:			**DEVELOPMENT OF IDEA:**		
Indenting			Title		
Margins			Facts		
Skipping Lines			Introduction		
Handwriting			Body		
Personal/Business Letter Form			Conclusion		
Poetry Form			Sequence		
Other: _____			Imagination		
Other: _____			Details		
			Conversation		
MECHANICS:			Description		
Capitalization			Personification		
Punctuation			Main Idea		
Spelling			Paragraphing		
Verb Tense			Rhyming		
Grammar			Rhythm		
Possessives			Other: _____		
Syllabication			Other: _____		
Complete Sentences			COMMENTS:		
Sentence Length					
Variety of Word Choice					
Other: _____					
Other: _____					

COMPOSITION EVALUATION

STUDENT: _____ DATE: _____

WRITING ASSIGNMENT: _____

EVALUATOR(S): _____

	Self-Evaluation YES NO	Peer Group Evaluation YES NO	Teacher's Comment
Content			
1. Is each word group a sentence?			
2. Is each sentence worded clearly?			
3. Are descriptive words used?			
4. Is the main idea clear?			
5. Are more sentences needed to tell about the main idea?			
Organization			
1. Does the composition have a clear beginning, middle and end?			
2. Are the ideas grouped into paragraphs?			
3. Are the sentences in a paragraph put in logical order? (Sequence)			
Mechanics			
1. Are capital letters used correctly?			
2. Are punctuation marks used correctly?			
3. Are words spelled correctly?			
4. Are tenses (present, past, or future) used appropriately throughout the composition?			
5. Is the handwriting neat and readable?			
Can this composition be improved?			
How can this composition be improved?			

Teacher: _____

Self: _____

Peer: _____

IC–12 **CRITICAL THINKING/INQUIRY SKILLS EVALUATION**

TEACHER: _____ DATE: _____

REFER TO *BLOOM'S TAXONOMY OF THINKING SKILLS* FOR AN EXPLANATION OF THE SIX LEVELS ON THIS FORM AND THEIR SUB-SKILLS.

Student	Knowledge	Comprehension	Application	Analysis	Synthesis	Evaluation
1)						
2)						
3)						
4)						
5)						
6)						
7)						
8)						
9)						
10)						
11)						
12)						
13)						
14)						
15)						
16)						
17)						
18)						
19)						
20)						
21)						
22)						
23)						
24)						
25)						
26)						
27)						

TEAM TEACHER'S EVALUATION

TEACHER TO: _____

TEACHER FROM: _____

SUBJECT: _____

Goal, Subject, etc. → Student's Name ↓							
1. _____							
2. _____							
3. _____							
4. _____							
5. _____							
6. _____							
7. _____							
8. _____							
9. _____							
10. _____							
11. _____							
12. _____							
13. _____							
14. _____							
15. _____							

COMMENTS:

To: _____
Classroom Teacher

Re: _____
Student

From: _____
Special Teacher

Date: _____

Subject Taught: _____

    Skills Worked on:

    Improvement Shown:

    More Work Needed:

Subject Taught: _____

    Skills Worked on:

    Improvement Shown:

    More Work Needed:

Subject Taught: _____

    Skills Worked on:

    Improvement Shown:

    More Work Needed:

Additional Comments: _____

_____

_____

_____

_____

Communicating
with
Colleagues

ID–1   PROFESSIONAL TELEPHONE DIRECTORY

SCHOOL: _____   YEAR: _____

Name	Telephone Number or Extension	Position

TEACHER MESSAGE FORM

TEACHERS: PLEASE PLACE YOUR INITIALS AFTER YOUR NAME ONCE YOU HAVE READ THE MESSAGE BELOW.

Names of Teachers	Message	
	Date:	**Time:**

ID–3

NEW CLASS INFORMATION SHEET

CURRENT TEACHER: _____

NEXT YEAR'S TEACHER: _____

NEXT YEAR'S GRADE: _____

Student's Name	Minority	Sex	Standard Test National %			R. Book Recommended Publ.-Title-Level	M. Book Recommended Publ.-Title-Level	Comments
			R	M	Sp.	L			
1.									
2.									
3.									
4.									
5.									
6.									
7.									
8.									
9.									
10.									
11.									
12.									
13.									
14.									
15.									
16.									
17.									
18.									
19.									
20.									
21.									
22.									
23.									
24.									
25.									
26.									
27.									

DISCIPLINE RECORD ID–4

Rules and Consequences should be clearly established with the student prior to use of this sheet.

Student's Name	Date	Infraction	Consequences

BACK-TO-SCHOOL NIGHT:
SUGGESTIONS FOR CLASSROOM PRESENTATION

To: Colleagues

From: _____
                    (Administrator)

Date: _____

Re: Back-to-School Night suggestions for classroom presentations

_____

I. Educational background of teacher:

II. Goals for the year (curricular goals, behavioral objectives, trips, etc.):

III. Classroom procedures and rules:

IV. How parents can help:

V. Parent/Teacher communication procedures:

ID–6 CLASSROOM TEACHER/SPECIALIST INFORMATION FORM

STUDENT: _____   CLASSROOM TEACHER: _____

GRADE: _____   RESOURCE ROOM TEACHER: _____

CLASSROOM UPDATE	Date:
Skills Currently Stressed:	
Difficulties:	
Successes:	
Additional Comments:	
Materials Needed:	

RESOURCE ROOM UPDATE	Date:
Skills Currently Stressed:	
Difficulties:	
Successes:	
Additional Comments:	
Materials Used:	

SAME-FAMILY CONFERENCE SCHEDULE

SCHOOL: _____ MONTH: _____ YEAR: _____

Teacher	Student	Date	Time

SCHOOL: _____ WEEK OF: _____

Monday, _____

Tuesday, _____

Wednesday, _____

Thursday, _____

Friday, _____

Important Upcoming Events:

FROM _____ SCHOOL TO YOUR HOUSE

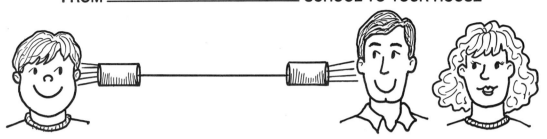

HAVING FUN WHILE LEARNING AT HOME

SCHOOL EVENTS

ADVICE COLUMN

BILL/RECEIPT FOR LOST MATERIAL

Billing Form

Date: _____

To: _____
(Parent)

From: _____   _____
(School)   (Authorized personnel)

Re: _____
(Lost or damaged material)

Publisher's cost of new material: $_____

You pay: $_____

Date due: _____

Make checks payable to: _____
(Name of School)

- -

Receipt of Payment Form

To: _____

From: _____

Payment for _____ has been received
(Lost or damaged material)

by _____, on _____
(Authorized personnel)   (Date)

Thank you.

ID–11

YEAR-END RECLASSIFICATION WORKSHEET

FOR CLASS: _____ FOR GRADE: _____ FOR YEAR: _____

Name	Sex	Academic Rank	Racial/Ethnic Minority	Classified	Level of Independence		
					High	Average	Low
1.							
2.							
3.							
4.							
5.							
6.							
7.							
8.							
9.							
10.							
11.							
12.							
13.							
14.							
15.							
16.							
17.							
18.							
19.							
20.							
21.							
22.							
23.							
24.							
25.							
26.							
27.							
Totals:	M	F					

ID–12   YEAR-END RECLASSIFICATION SHEET FOR GROUPING

TEACHER: _____   GRADE: _____   SCHOOL YEAR: _____

Name	Basal Reader Completed Publisher-Title-Level	Spelling Book Completed Publisher-Title-Level	Math Book Completed Publisher-Title-Level	Standardized Test Scores			
				Total Reading	Total Math	Total Spelling	Total Lang.
1.							
2.							
3.							
4.							
5.							
6.							
7.							
8.							
9.							
10.							
11.							
12.							
13.							
14.							
15.							
16.							
17.							
18.							
19.							
20.							
21.							
22.							
23.							
24.							
25.							
26.							
27.							

ID–13 YEAR-END RECLASSIFICATION SUMMARY SHEET

Grade: _____

School: _____

Teacher: _____

School Year of: _____

Number of Boys . . . . • _____

Number of Girls. . . . . • _____

    Total Pupils. . . . . • _____

Number of Minority. . . . . • _____

Number of Leaders. . . . . • _____

Number of Behavioral Problems. . . . _____

Number of Learning Problems. . . . . _____

Number of Reluctant Workers . . . . . _____

Number of Classified. . . . . _____

Number of Speech Children . . . . . • _____

Number of Basic Skills . . . . • _____

Number of Gifted Nominees . . . . . • _____

<table>
<tr><td colspan="2" style="text-align:center">Children to be Separated from Each Other:</td></tr>
<tr><td>_____ From</td><td>_____</td></tr>
<tr><td>_____ From</td><td>_____</td></tr>
<tr><td>_____ From</td><td>_____</td></tr>
<tr><td>_____ From</td><td>_____</td></tr>
</table>

List reading scores
from highest to lowest:

1. _____
2. _____
3. _____
4. _____
5. _____
6. _____
7. _____
8. _____
9. _____
10. _____
11. _____
12. _____
13. _____
14. _____
15. _____
16. _____
17. _____
18. _____
19. _____
20. _____
21. _____
22. _____
23. _____
24. _____
25. _____
26. _____
27. _____
28. _____

FORMS TO USE
WITH STUDENTS

Helping students organize their time and materials provides the basis for their personal growth and development. Structuring the curriculum gives them clear and consistent expectations, which encourages and enhances their scholastic growth. Given the means, most students begin to develop independence of thought and process.

EXPLANATORY NOTES

Form IIA–10: Tailor assignments to fit the needs of students. Examples include guide words, pronunciation, page location, syllables, meaning, and alphabetizing.

Form IIA–27: Questions will vary depending on the purpose of the interview. Students may tape the interviews and then write notes from the tape.

Form IIB–7: In each square, write a student's name and the assignment(s) you want him or her to complete.

Form IIC–2: This is for primary grades.

Form IIC–3: This is for primary grades.

Form IIC–4: This is for intermediate grades. See "Weekly Schedule Sample" (Form IB–12) and "Absentee's Homework Assignment Sheet" (Form IIB–3).

Form IIC–5: This is for intermediate grades.

Form IIC–10: This form can be used to list the names of students who are helpers in the classroom or in the school.

Form IIC–12: You might want to put a sticker in the center of the award.

Form IIC–14: This is a contribution appreciation form.

Form IIC–15: This is a certificate of participation.

Structuring Curriculum

STUDENT INTEREST INVENTORY

NAME: _____ DATE: _____ GRADE: _____

1. What games do you like to play? _____
   _____
   _____

2. What do you like to make? _____
   _____

3. What kind of pet(s) do you have? _____
   _____

4. Do you belong to any clubs? _____ Which ones? _____
   _____

5. Do you take any special lessons? _____
   _____

6. What things do you collect? _____
   _____

7. What are your favorite television programs? _____
   _____

8. What is the best book you ever read? _____
   _____

9. What other books have you liked? _____
   _____

10. Do you like to listen to stories? _____

11. Do you read to anyone? _____

12. Do you have a library card? _____

13. How often do you go to the library? _____

14. Do you read magazines, comics or newspapers? _____
   _____

15. What kind of work to you want to do when you finish school (in your adult life)? ____
   _____
   _____
   _____
   _____

STUDENT INTERVIEW

TEACHER: _____ DATE: _____

STUDENT'S NAME: _____

1. What subject or subjects do you like?

   Reading _____   Social Studies _____

   Math _____   Creative Writing _____

   Science _____   Art _____

   Music _____   Computer _____

   Gym _____   Other _____

2. What would you like to be able to do in class this year?

   _____

   _____

   _____

   _____

   _____

   _____

   _____

   _____

3. What subject or subjects do you think you are especially good at?

   Reading _____   Social Studies _____

   Math _____   Creative Writing _____

   Science _____   Art _____

   Music _____   Computer _____

   Gym _____   Other _____

4. What subject or subjects do you find most difficult for you?

   Reading _____   Social Studies _____

   Math _____   Creative Writing _____

   Science _____   Art _____

   Music _____   Computer _____

   Gym _____   Other _____

5. What do you like doing for a project?

Oral Reports	_____	Drawings	_____
Dioramas	_____	Displays	_____
Experiments	_____	Maps	_____
Collages	_____	Written Reports	_____
Mobiles	_____	Puppet Shows	_____
Plays	_____	Debates	_____
Other	_____	Other	_____

6. How many special friends do you have in this class? _____

    Who are they: _____

_____

7. Have you had problems with any students in this class? _____

    If you have had a problem what is it? _____

_____

_____

8 If you were the teacher what subject or subjects would you like to teach?

Reading	_____	Social Studies	_____
Math	_____	Creative Writing	_____
Science	_____	Art	_____
Music	_____	Computer	_____
Gym	_____	Other	_____

9. If you could change anything you wanted to in this class to make it better, what would it be? _____

_____

_____

_____

10. Is there anything else you would like to tell me? Write about it in the space below.

_____

_____

_____

_____

IIA–3

MOTIVATION FORM

NAME: _____

BEGINNING DATE: _____

ENDING DATE: _____

As you complete each assignment, color every red stripe or draw one row of stars. Study our classroom flag in order to copy it accurately. Sixteen finished assignments will complete a flag.

MULTI-ASSIGNMENT REMINDER

NAME: _____ DATE: _____

The assignments named below have been explained in detail to you. Please work on them thoughout the _____.
(Time Period)

Ask questions if you need to. Each assignment will be accepted at school as you complete it. All are due by _____.

    1. _____

    2. _____

    3. _____

    4. _____

- -

MULTI-ASSIGNMENT REMINDER

NAME: _____ DATE: _____

The assignments named below have been explained in detail to you. Please work on them thoughout the _____.
(Time Period)

Ask questions if you need to. Each assignment will be accepted at school as you complete it. All are due by _____.

    1. _____

    2. _____

    3. _____

    4. _____

COMPREHENSION QUIZ FORM

NAME: _____ DATE: _____

Book: _____ Story: _____

1. _____
2. _____
3. _____
4. _____
5. _____
6. _____
7. _____
8. _____
9. _____
10. _____

- -

COMPREHENSION QUIZ FORM

NAME: _____ DATE: _____

Book: _____ Story: _____

1. _____
2. _____
3. _____
4. _____
5. _____
6. _____
7. _____
8. _____
9. _____
10. _____

SPELLING LIST FORM

NAME: _____   DATE: _____

SPELLING LIST NO. _____

STUDY METHOD

1. Look at the word. Say it.

2. Close your eyes. Think what the word looks like. Say the word. Spell the word aloud.

3. Open your eyes. Look at the word again. Were you right? If you made a mistake, go back and do Step 1 and Step 2 again.

4. Cover the word. Write the word. Did you spell it right? If you made a mistake, go back and do Step 1 and Step 2 again.

5. Cover the word you just wrote. Write it again two more times.

1.	1.	1.
2.	2.	2.
3.	3.	3.
4.	4.	4.
5.	5.	5.
6.	6.	6.
7.	7.	7.
8.	8.	8.
9.	9.	9.
10.	10.	10.
11.	11.	11.
12.	12.	12.
13.	13.	13.
14.	14.	14.
15.	15.	15.
16.	16.	16.
17.	17.	17.
18.	18.	18.
19.	19.	19.
20.	20.	20.

WEEKLY SPELLING TEST FORM

IIA–7

NAME: _____ GRADE: _____ ROOM: _____

DATE: _____

BOOK: _____ LESSON NUMBER: _____

1. _____   11. _____
2. _____   12. _____
3. _____   13. _____
4. _____   14. _____
5. _____   15. _____
6. _____   16. _____
7. _____   17. _____
8. _____   18. _____
9. _____   19. _____
10. _____   20. _____

Possible Number Right: _____

Number Right: _____

Percent Right: _____

© 1989 by Parker Publishing Company

95

UNIT SPELLING TEST FORM

NAME: _____

DATE: _____ GRADE: _____ ROOM: _____

BOOK: _____ UNIT NUMBER: _____

1. _____

2. _____

3. _____

4. _____

5. _____

6. _____

7. _____

8. _____

9. _____

10. _____

11. _____

12. _____

13. _____

14. _____

15. _____

16. _____

17. _____

18. _____

19. _____

20. _____

21. _____

22. _____

23. _____

24. _____

25. _____

Possible Number Right: _____

Number Right: _____

Percent Right: _____

NAME: _____ DATE: _____

Word/Pronunciation	Part of Speech	Definition	My Sentence
1)			
2)			
3)			
4)			
5)			
6)			
7)			
8)			

DICTIONARY FORM

NAME: _____ DATE: _____

ENTRY WORDS	ASSIGNMENTS

NAME: _____ DATE: _____

Word	Original Spelling	Place of Origin	Definitions (Old and New)

NAME: _____ DATE: _____

My classmate _____ listened to my
(Student's Name)

_____ called _____
(Story, Poem, Report, etc.)

and suggested _____

_____

_____

_____

_____

_____

_____

_____

_____

My teacher _____ listened to my
(Teacher's Name)

_____ called _____
(Story, Poem, Report, etc.)

and suggested _____

_____

_____

_____

_____

_____

_____

_____

NAME: _____ DATE: _____

GOALS: _____

_____

(Indent) → _____

_____

_____

_____

_____

_____

_____

_____

_____

_____

_____

_____

_____

_____

_____

_____

Tally of capitalization mistakes:	Tally of punctuation mistakes:	Tally of spelling mistakes:
Words added or left out (number of times):	Congratulations! You arrived at your goal(s)!	Try harder.

HOLISTIC COMPOSITION EVALUATION

AUTHOR: _____

EVALUATOR: _____

COMPOSITION TITLE: _____

Areas to Assess	Rating				
Ideas and Content	1	2	3	4	5
Structure and Organization	1	2	3	4	5
Grammar and Usage	1	2	3	4	5
Capitalization, Punctuation, Spelling	1	2	3	4	5

1=Unsatisfactory   2=Fair   3=Satisfactory   4=Good   5=Excellent

Strengths: _____

_____

_____

_____

_____

Weaknesses: _____

_____

_____

_____

_____

Other Comments: _____

_____

_____

_____

_____

_____

_____

HEADING

```
_____
        Number and Street
_____
      Town, State, Zip Code
_____
              Date
```

Dear _____,
                Greeting

```
_____
_____
_____
_____
_____
_____
_____
_____
```

BODY

```
_____,
         Closing

_____
         Signature
```

PERSONAL
HEADING

Number and Street

Town, State, Zip Code

Date

Person

Title of Company

Number and Street

BUSINESS
HEADING

Town, State, Zip Code

Dear _____ ;

Greeting

BODY

Closing

Signature

PLAYWRITING FORM

TITLE: _____ AUTHOR(S): _____
_____
_____

Characters:

_____   _____

_____   _____

_____   _____

_____   _____

_____   _____

- -

Setting: _____

Time: _____ Place: _____

_____:_____
(Character)

_____

_____

_____

_____:_____
(Character)

_____

_____

_____

_____:_____
(Character)

_____

_____

_____

_____:_____
(Character)

_____

_____

_____

——————————————: ————————————————————
(Character)

——————————————————————————————————————

——————————————————————————————————————

——————————————————————————————————————

——————————————: ————————————————————
(Character)

——————————————————————————————————————

——————————————————————————————————————

——————————————————————————————————————

——————————————: ————————————————————
(Character)

——————————————————————————————————————

——————————————————————————————————————

——————————————————————————————————————

——————————————: ————————————————————
(Character)

——————————————————————————————————————

——————————————————————————————————————

——————————————————————————————————————

——————————————: ————————————————————
(Character)

——————————————————————————————————————

——————————————————————————————————————

——————————————————————————————————————

——————————————: ————————————————————
(Character)

——————————————————————————————————————

——————————————————————————————————————

——————————————————————————————————————

——————————————: ————————————————————
(Character)

——————————————————————————————————————

——————————————————————————————————————

BOOK REPORT FORM

NAME: _____ DATE: _____

_____
Title

_____
Author (Last name first)

_____ _____
Publisher   Copyright date

Type of Book: _____
(Fiction, Non-Fiction, Biography, etc.)

1. (Question to answer) _____

_____

_____

2. _____

_____

_____

_____

3. _____

_____

_____

_____

4. _____

_____

_____

_____

5. Drawing

NAME: _____ GRADE: _____

I have finished reading:

Title of Book	Author's Last Name	Date Completed
The book I liked best on this paper is: **Title**	**Author**	**Date Completed**

MY READING-BY-CATEGORY CHART

NAME: _____

GRADE: _____

Be a well-rounded reader. Write the title or shade one section for each book you've finished reading.

FICTION	ART	MUSIC	HISTORY	HOW TO
SPORTS	MYSTERY	BIOGRAPHY	SCIENCE	SCIENCE FICTION

MY AT-HOME-READING CALENDAR

IIA–22

NAME: _____

MONTH: _____

a. Title
b. Listener
c. Minutes Read Aloud

	SUNDAY	MONDAY	TUESDAY	WEDNESDAY	THURSDAY	FRIDAY	SATURDAY
Week of	a. b. c.	a. b. c.	a. b. c.	a. b. c.	a. b. c.	a. b. c.	a. b. c.
Week of	a. b. c.	a. b. c.	a. b. c.	a. b. c.	a. b. c.	a. b. c.	a. b. c.
Week of	a. b. c.	a. b. c.	a. b. c.	a. b. c.	a. b. c.	a. b. c.	a. b. c.
Week of	a. b. c.	a. b. c.	a. b. c.	a. b. c.	a. b. c.	a. b. c.	a. b. c.

PLANNING A REPORT

NAME: _____ DATE ASSIGNED: _____

TEACHER: _____ DATE DUE: _____

1. My assignment is: _____

   _____

   _____

2. My report should be approximately _____ pages long.

3. I need information on _____
   Examples: giraffe, habitat, food, protection, young, etc.

   _____

4. Some questions I must answer in my report are: _____

   _____

   _____

   _____

   _____

   _____

5. Places I should look for information are: _____

   _____

   _____

   _____

   Examples: dictionaries, encyclopedias, card catalogue, pictures, maps, filmstrips,
             videocassettes, etc.

6. These are the titles of the materials that I might use: _____

   _____

   _____

   _____

   _____

   _____

Name: _____ Date: _____

The title of my report is _____.

Subtopics I need to read about are:

_____ _____ _____

_____ _____ _____

One good source of information is:

Title: _____ Volume: _____ Number: _____

Author: _____

Publisher: _____

Copyright Date: _____ Pages: _____

Directions: Use each box below to take notes pertaining to *one* subtopic as you read about it in the source named above. Remember! Copy only key words or phrases. Add your own words.

Subtopic:
Notes:

Subtopic:
Notes:

Subtopic:
Notes:

MAKING AN OUTLINE

An outline is a form for putting together information and ideas so that the most important ideas are placed in headings followed by related but less important information.

Outline of main ideas (the most important ones)

I. _____

II. _____

III. _____

Next take each important idea from above and add related details, using as many subheadings as you need.

I. _____

  A. _____

    1. _____

      a. _____

      b. _____

    2. _____

  B. _____

    1. _____

    2. _____

II. _____

  A. _____

  B. _____

III. _____

  A. _____

    1. _____

    2. _____

  B. _____

A bibliography is a list of the references you use to get information for your report. References are usually books, parts of books, encyclopedias and magazine articles.

As soon as you find information for your report in a reference write these down in the following order: the name of the author (last name first), the name of the book, the publisher's name, the date of publication, and the page numbers.

If the reference does not have an author begin with the first word in the title.

Below are sample listings for each type of reference. Pay close attention to capitalization and punctuation.

A Book

    Mason, Jeffrey R. Alaska. Houghton Mifflin, 1985.

Part of a Book

    Smith, Margaret and Daniels, Sara. Painting Flowers. Anderson and Company, 1986, pp. 101–124.

Encyclopedia Article

    Woodchuck, Britannica Junior Encyclopedia, 1985, Vol. 17, pp. 62–64.

Magazine Article

    Farrell, Jonas. "The Berbers of Morocco." National Geographic, October 1987, pp. 572–577.

    How to prepare a sample bibliography on this topic: _____

_____

    A Book: _____

_____

    Part of a Book: _____

_____

    Encyclopedia Article: _____

_____

    Magazine Article: _____

_____

Once you have completed the above information about each of your references, combine them in one list, called a bibliography. Arrange each reference in alphabetical order by the first word in each entry.

INTERVIEW NOTES

NAME: _____ TOPIC: _____

NAME OF PERSON INTERVIEWING: _____

REASON FOR INTERVIEW: _____

Questions I will ask: _____

    1. _____

    2. _____

    3. _____

    4. _____

    5. _____

    6. _____

Notes from my interview with: _____

_____

_____

_____

_____

_____

_____

_____

_____

_____

_____

_____

_____

_____

_____

_____

_____

_____

NAME: _____ DATE DUE: _____

1. Several days before it is due have a grown-up in your family help you choose an interesting article that you can understand. Read it aloud together.

2. Choose nothing about fire, accident, death or other violent act unless it happens to a famous person.

3. Fill in the information on the form below.

4. On the back of this paper write two interesting facts in addition to the answers below. Use sentences when you write them.

5. Practice saying the facts from memory several times.

6. Bring to school the whole article and this paper on the day they are due. Give them to your teacher. Stand in front of the class and explain the article from memory loudly and clearly.

- -

Who? _____

What? _____

_____

When? _____

Where? _____

How? or Why? _____

_____

_____

_____

_____

_____

_____

_____

_____

_____

NAME: _____

DATE: _____   GRADE: _____   ROOM: _____

SUBJECT: _____   CURRENT EVENT ASSIGNMENT _____

My next presentation will take place on: _____

Name of newspaper or magazine: _____

Date of newspaper or magazine: _____

Title of article: _____

About whom is the article? _____

What is the most important thing that happened? _____

_____

_____

_____

When did it happen? _____

Where did it happen? _____

How or why did it happen? _____

_____

_____

_____

Write another interesting fact: _____

_____

_____

_____

_____

Write still another interesting fact: _____

_____

_____

_____

_____

_____   _____

Student's Name   Grade

_____

Teacher's Name

_____   _____   _____

Title of Experiment   Date Begun   Date Concluded

Date	Record of Observations

_____   _____   _____

Title of Experiment   Date Begun   Date Concluded

Date	Record of Observations

SCIENCE EXPERIMENT

NAME: _____ DATE: _____

TEACHER: _____ GRADE: _____

1. Objective(s) of experiment: _____

_____

_____

_____

2. Material(s) needed: _____

_____

_____

3. Procedure(s) to be followed: _____

_____

_____

_____

_____

4. Result(s) observed: _____

_____

_____

_____

_____

5. Conclusions drawn from observation(s): _____

_____

_____

_____

_____

_____

Date: _____   Date: _____
            Begun   Finished

STUDENT'S NAME: _____   WEEK OF: _____

Title of Center	What I Did
1)	
2)	
3)	
4)	
5)	
6)	
7)	
8)	
9)	
10)	

LEARNING CENTER FORM—GROUP

Title or Subject: _____

Dear Student: After you work in this center today please write your name, the date and what you did. Thank you.

My Name	Date	What I Did Today in this Center

NAME: _____ DATE: _____

Directions: Use each box to write the complete family of facts
(+, −) or (×, ÷) for any given equation. The first
box holds an example.

2 + 1 = 3	1 + 2 = 3	3 − 1 = 2	3 − 2 = 1

IIA–35

NAME: _____

MATH MOUNTAIN

Start with _____ and _____ _____ each time.
            (Number)   (Operation) (Number)

PROGRAM: _____   DATE: _____

SUBJECT: _____   STUDENT'S NAME: _____

1. Did you enjoy the program? _____

    Why? _____

    _____

    _____

    _____

2. What did you learn from the program? _____

    _____

    _____

    _____

    _____

    _____

3. What did you know about the subject before you saw the program? _____

    _____

    _____

    _____

4. Would you like to write _____,

    read _____, or make _____

    about the program? _____

    _____

STUDENT'S FIELD TRIP PROCEDURES

STUDENT'S NAME: _____

TRIP TO: _____

DATE: _____

1. Your group leader is _____.

   Your buddy is _____.

   Remain with your assigned group at all times.

2. Be courteous to everyone.

3. Listen to and follow directions quickly. They are given with your safety and enjoyment in mind.

4. It is suggested that you wear _____

   _____.

5. Please bring with you _____

   _____

   _____

   _____.

6. Please do not bring _____

   _____

   _____

   _____.

7. Be responsible for your own belongings.

8. Be prepared to tell what you learned when we discuss the trip in class.

BE SAFE AND ENJOY THE TRIP

Organizing Student Time and Materials

INDIVIDUALIZED WEEKLY SCHEDULE

STUDENT'S NAME: _____ HOMEROOM TEACHER: _____

CODE: Art=A   Music=M   Phys. Ed.=P.E.   Library Media Center = L.M.C.

Math=Math   Language Arts=L.A.   Reading=Rd.   Social Studies = S.S.

Science=Sc. Health=H.   Computer=C.   Writing Workshop=W.W.

TIME	MONDAY	TUESDAY	WEDNESDAY	THURSDAY	FRIDAY	
	L	U	N	C	H	

Other Areas of Instruction	Time(s)	Day(s)

NAME: _____   DATE: _____

- -

Subject: _____

Assignment: _____

Time Worked in School: _____   Time Worked at Home: _____

- -

Subject: _____

Assignment: _____

Time Worked in School: _____   Time Worked at Home: _____

- -

Subject: _____

Assignment: _____

Time Worked in School: _____   Time Worked at Home: _____

- -

Subject: _____

Assignment: _____

Time Worked in School: _____   Time Worked at Home: _____

- -

	Yes	I Need to Improve
Did I understand the assignments?	_____	_____
Did I estimate correctly the amount of time I'd need?	_____	_____
Did I organize my time in school?	_____	_____
Did I organize my time at home?	_____	_____
Did I proofread completed work?	_____	_____
Did I work quickly and carefully?	_____	_____

IIB–3 ABSENTEE'S HOMEWORK ASSIGNMENT SHEET

NAME: _____ DATE: _____

PHONE NUMBER: _____

NAME OF HOMEWORK PARTNER (IN CLASS OF ABSENTEE): _____

NAME OF PERSON TO TAKE HOME: _____

READING _____

_____

HANDWRITING _____

SPELLING _____

ENGLISH _____

MATH _____

SOCIAL STUDIES _____

SCIENCE _____

CURRENT EVENTS _____

WRITING WORKSHOP _____

OTHER _____

OTHER _____

OTHER _____

BOOKS NEEDED:

READING _____ SPELLING _____

MATH _____ SCIENCE _____

SOCIAL STUDIES _____ OTHER _____

OTHER _____ OTHER _____

NAME: _____

WEEK OF: _____ GRADE: _____ ROOM: _____

I must practice: _____

    I practiced Monday for   _____ minutes.

    I practiced Tuesday for   _____ minutes.

    I practiced Wednesday for   _____ minutes.

    I practiced Thursday for   _____ minutes.

    I practiced Friday for   _____ minutes.

    I practiced Saturday for   _____ minutes.

    I practiced Sunday for   _____ minutes.

- -

PRACTICE ASSIGNMENT SHEET

NAME: _____

WEEK OF: _____ GRADE: _____ ROOM: _____

I must practice: _____

    I practiced Monday for   _____ minutes.

    I practiced Tuesday for   _____ minutes.

    I practiced Wednesday for   _____ minutes.

    I practiced Thursday for   _____ minutes.

    I practiced Friday for   _____ minutes.

    I practiced Saturday for   _____ minutes.

    I practiced Sunday for   _____ minutes.

MY INDEPENDENT WORK CONTRACT

NAME: _____ DATE: _____

I have work in _____. I need to _____
                    Subject(s)

_____

_____

I have work in _____. I need to _____
                    Subject(s)

_____

_____

I have work in _____. I need to _____
                    Subject(s)

_____

_____

- -

MY INDEPENDENT WORK CONTRACT

NAME: _____ DATE: _____

I have work in _____. I need to _____
                    Subject(s)

_____

_____

I have work in _____. I need to _____
                    Subject(s)

_____

_____

I have work in _____. I need to _____
                    Subject(s)

_____

_____

NAME: _____ DATE ASSIGNED: _____

SUBJECT: _____ DATE OF TEST: _____

  I. What to study: _____

_____

_____

_____

_____

_____

 II. How to study: _____

_____

_____

_____

_____

III. When to study: _____

_____

_____

_____

_____

IV. Materials I will need in order to study: _____

_____

_____

_____

 V. For help in studying I can ask: _____

_____

_____

_____

INDIVIDUALIZED PLANNING CHART

Directions: Place an X through your square when all your work is done.

(Student's Name)				

MONTH OF: _____   YEAR: _____

MONDAY	TUESDAY	WEDNESDAY	THURSDAY	FRIDAY

BUILDING PASS

_____ from _____ class
Student's Name   Teacher's Name

to _____. Left room at _____.
                                                                            Time

- -

BUILDING PASS

_____ from _____ class
Student's Name   Teacher's Name

to _____. Left room at _____.
                                                                            Time

- -

BUILDING PASS

_____ from _____ class
Student's Name   Teacher's Name

to _____. Left room at _____.
                                                                            Time

- -

BUILDING PASS

_____ from _____ class
Student's Name   Teacher's Name

to _____. Left room at _____.
                                                                            Time

- -

BUILDING PASS

_____ from _____ class
Student's Name   Teacher's Name

to _____. Left room at _____.
                                                                            Time

- -

BUILDING PASS

_____ from _____ class
Student's Name   Teacher's Name

to _____. Left room at _____.
                                                                            Time

ORGANIZING FOR ASSIGNMENTS CHECKLIST IIB-10

At School   **At Home**

_____
My Name

_____   I have pencils and pens.   _____

_____   I have a pencil sharpener.   _____

_____   I have erasers.   _____

_____   I have a ruler.   _____

_____   I have crayons and markers.   _____

_____   I have tape.   _____

_____   I have a notebook and/or paper.   _____

_____   I have a dictionary.   _____

_____   I have the books and other special materials (magazines,   _____
               construction paper, etc.) to complete my assignment.

_____   I have a quiet place to work.   _____

_____   I give myself enough time to complete assignments   _____
               when due.

_____   I am neat in my work and workplace.   _____

_____   I have good lighting.   _____

_____   I have a special place at home to put notices for my   _____
               parents to see.

_____   I have everything that I need to take to school/home   _____
               in one place.

Personal Growth and Development

CLASSROOM RULES FORM FOR STUDENTS

NAME: _____ DATE: _____

Written below are the rules for Schoolwork, Homework, and Behavior that we developed together. By making every effort to follow them, the school year will be better for all of us.

_____
Teacher

CLASSROOM RULES ON SCHOOLWORK

1. _____

2. _____

3. _____

4. _____

CLASSROOM RULES ON HOMEWORK

1. _____

2. _____

3. _____

4. _____

CLASSROOM RULES ON BEHAVIOR

1. _____

2. _____

3. _____

4. _____

I will pay attention.

I will follow directions.

I will wait my turn.

I will be polite.

I will finish my work.

I will take notes and notices home.

I will do my homework.

I will leave toys home.

I will bring important things to school.

Signed by Me: _____

Signed by My Teacher: _____

Date: _____

IIC–3   MY RESPONSIBILITIES SELF-EVALUATION—PRIMARY

NAME: _____   DATE: _____

DIRECTIONS: CIRCLE ONE CHOICE FOR EACH ITEM.

HERE IS HOW WELL I THINK I'M DOING:

I pay attention.	Poor	Fair	Great
I follow directions.	Poor	Fair	Great
I wait my turn.	Poor	Fair	Great
I am polite.	Poor	Fair	Great
I finish my work.	Poor	Fair	Great
I take notes and notices home.	Poor	Fair	Great
I do my homework.	Poor	Fair	Great
I leave toys home.	Poor	Fair	Great
I bring important things to school.	Poor	Fair	Great

1. I will listen to my teachers and my parents as they help me to plan and organize my time.

2. I will hang our Weekly Schedule in a place at home where I can always find it.

3. I will use the Weekly Schedule to help me plan my work, especially long-range assignments.

4. I will complete assignments on time so that I do not fall behind in my work.

5. I will accept the appropriate consequences if I am unprepared.

6. If I miss a lesson in school because of another activity I will ask a trustworthy person what I missed and do what is necessary to catch up.

7. If I miss assignments because I am absent, I know that my Assignment Partner has written them down for me.

8. I will make sure my parents receive notes and notices.

9. I will take necessary materials to school when they are required.

10. I understand that I may call home only in an emergency.

Signed by Me: _____ Date: _____

Signed by My Teacher: _____ Date: _____

IIC–5   MY RESPONSIBILITIES SELF-EVALUATION—INTERMEDIATE

NAME: _____   DATE: _____

DIRECTIONS: CIRCLE ONE CHOICE FOR EACH ITEM.

1. I listen to my teachers and my parents as they help me to plan and organize my time.
    All the Time   Sometimes   Almost Never

2. I have placed our Weekly Schedule in a place at home where I can always find it.
    All the Time   Sometimes   Almost Never

3. I use the Weekly Schedule to help me plan my work, especially long-range assignments.
    All the Time   Sometimes   Almost Never

4. I complete assignments on time so that I do not fall behind in my work.
    All the Time   Sometimes   Almost Never

5. I accept the appropriate consequences if I am unprepared.
    All the Time   Sometimes   Almost Never

6. When I've missed a lesson in school because of another activity I have asked a trustworthy person what I missed and do what is necessary to catch up.
    All the Time   Sometimes   Almost Never

7. When I've missed assignments because I am absent I know that my assignment partner has written them down for me.
    All the Time   Sometimes   Almost Never

8. I make sure my parents receive notes and notices.
    All the Time   Sometimes   Almost Never

9. I take necessary materials to school when they are required.
    All the Time   Sometimes   Almost Never

10. I call home only in an emergency.
    All the Time   Sometimes   Almost Never

Signed by Me: _____   Date: _____

Signed by My Teacher: _____   Date: _____

IIC–6

SELF-EVALUATION SHEET—MULTIPURPOSE

NAME: _____   DATE: _____

I'VE CIRCLED HOW I THINK I'M DOING IN:

_____	Not-So-Well	Just O.K.	Good	Super
_____	Not-So-Well	Just O.K.	Good	Super
_____	Not-So-Well	Just O.K.	Good	Super
_____	Not-So-Well	Just O.K.	Good	Super
_____	Not-So-Well	Just O.K.	Good	Super
_____	Not-So-Well	Just O.K.	Good	Super
_____	Not-So-Well	Just O.K.	Good	Super
_____	Not-So-Well	Just O.K.	Good	Super
_____	Not-So-Well	Just O.K.	Good	Super
_____	Not-So-Well	Just O.K.	Good	Super
_____	Not-So-Well	Just O.K.	Good	Super

STUDENT BEHAVIOR CONTRACT

NAME: _____ DATE: _____

1. I will be polite to my teacher(s).

2. I will be polite to my classmates.

3. I will tell my teacher(s) if someone is bothering me.

4. I will walk, not run, in the hallways and on the stairs.

5. I will be quiet during fire drills.

6. I will be quiet in the hallways, on the stairs and during assemblies.

7. I will work and play cooperatively in class and on the playground.

_____
Signed by Me

_____
Signed by My Teacher

IIC–8   PERSONALIZED HOME AND SCHOOL BEHAVIOR MODIFICATION CONTRACT (SAMPLE)

PERSONAL CONTRACT OF _____
(Student's Name)

WEEK OF: _____

DID I:	MONDAY	TUESDAY	WEDNESDAY	THURSDAY	FRIDAY
Return all papers to school this morning?					
Bring all my homework home this evening?					
Hang up my coat and put away my bookbag?					
Wash my face and hands?					
Clean up the kitchen after a snack?					
Do my homework?					
Clean up my room?					
TOTAL POINTS					

We developed this contract together and agree to abide by it: _____
(Child's Signature)

_____
(Teacher's Signature)

_____
(Parent's Signature)

Point System
30–35 points = Excellent = Outside entertainment or toy
25–30 points = Good   = T.V.
20–25 points = Fair   = Dessert
 0–20 points = Disaster = Nothing
Each success for each day is worth one point.

IIC–9 PERSONALIZED IN-SCHOOL BEHAVIOR MODIFICATION CONTRACT
(SAMPLE)

NAME: _____   WEEK OF: _____

TEACHER'S SIGNATURE: _____

STUDENT'S SIGNATURE: _____

	MONDAY	TUESDAY	WEDNESDAY	THURSDAY	FRIDAY	TOTAL
A.						
B.						
C.						
D.						
E.						
F.						

A. PENCIL: 5 pts. per day
B. READING ASSIGNMENTS: 5 pts.
    3 × per week
C. ARGUMENTS: 5 pts. off per
    day (1 pt. per argument)

D. NEATNESS: 2 pts. per day
E. MATH: 5 pts. per day
F. SPELLING: 5 pts. twice a week

TOTAL POSSIBLE POINTS PER WEEK: 100

(School Year)

_____
(Title of Position
example: Library Assistants)

1. _____
2. _____
3. _____
4. _____
5. _____

(Title of Position)

1. _____
2. _____
3. _____
4. _____
5. _____

(Title of Position)

1. _____
2. _____
3. _____
4. _____
5. _____

(Title of Position)

1. _____
2. _____
3. _____
4. _____
5. _____

(Title of Position)

1. _____
2. _____
3. _____
4. _____
5. _____

(Title of Position)

1. _____
2. _____
3. _____
4. _____
5. _____

_____
(Teacher's Name)

_____
(Grade)

SUCCESS CERTIFICATE

_____ IS A SUCCESS!!

_____

_____

_____

_____

TEACHER: _____

DATE: _____

- -

SUCCESS CERTIFICATE

_____ IS A SUCCESS!!

_____

_____

_____

_____

TEACHER: _____

DATE: _____

YOUR BEHAVIOR
HAS BEEN
SUPER!

THIS AWARD PRESENTED TO

_____

NAME OF STUDENT

_____

Classroom Teacher's Signature   Date

- -

YOUR BEHAVIOR
HAS BEEN
SUPER!

THIS AWARD PRESENTED TO

_____

NAME OF STUDENT

_____

Classroom Teacher's Signature   Date

CERTIFICATE
OF
MERIT
IS AWARDED TO

_____

NAME OF STUDENT

FOR _____

_____   _____
Classroom Teacher's Signature   Other Signature

DATE: _____

- -

CERTIFICATE
OF
MERIT
IS AWARDED TO

_____

NAME OF STUDENT

FOR _____

_____   _____
Classroom Teacher's Signature   Other Signature

DATE: _____

It is with **APPRECIATION** that we recognize the **CONTRIBUTION**

Made by _____
(Person or Group)

Of _____
(Description)

TO THE STUDENT COUNCIL'S

_____ PROJECT

DURING THE _____ SCHOOL YEAR

_____	_____
SCHOOL	STUDENT COUNCIL PRESIDENT
_____	_____
TOWN	STUDENT COUNCIL ADVISOR
_____	_____
STATE	PRINCIPAL

This is to certify that

_____

(NAME OF STUDENT)

**has successfully and diligently
served on the**

_____

of

_____

(NAME OF SCHOOL)

Advisor _____

for the year _____ Principal _____

- -

This is to certify that

_____

(NAME OF STUDENT)

**has successfully and diligently
served on the**

_____

of

_____

(NAME OF SCHOOL)

Advisor _____

for the year _____ Principal _____

FORMS FOR COMMUNICATING WITH PARENTS

Communicating effectively with parents is of prime importance in order to foster a good working relationship and garner their respect and support. When parents know and understand what is happening throughout the year in the classroom relative to expectations, goals, activities, ways to help children at home, assignments, and conferences, questions of accountability are answered before they arise and the teacher is protected.

EXPLANATORY NOTES

Form IIIA–6: The brochure mentioned could include Forms IIIA–8 through IIIA–14.

Form IIIA–9: Item 2 refers to Form IIIA–12.

Form IIIA–13: This is for primary grades.

Form IIIA–14: This is for intermediate grades.

Form IIIC–4: This form can be used to collate information gathered from "Survey of Parent Resources" (Form IIIC–3.)

Informing
Parents

Date _____

Dear _____,

It is with pleasure that I welcome you and _____ to the _____ grade this year. Cooperatively we can provide an educational environment which will enhance _____'s learning experiences. With mutual respect and continued efforts through frequent communication, he/she should grow both academically and personally during this school year.

I look forward to meeting you at Back-to-School Night when you'll receive information explaining our educational goals.

If at any time you wish to discuss _____'s progress, please call to arrange a convenient appointment. It is important that we work together in _____'s best interest.

Sincerely yours,

_____

PARENT'S PERSONAL DATA REQUEST FORM   IIIA–2

Date _____

Dear Parent,

    It is very important for _____'s welfare that we have
updated information about you. Please fill in the required data below.
    Thank you for your cooperation.

_____
                                Teacher

PERSONAL DATA (For school use only):

Name: _____

Present address: _____

_____

_____

Home telephone: _____

Work telephone: (Mother) _____ (Hours) _____

(Father) _____ (Hours) _____

(Custodial Guardian) _____ (Hours) _____

In case of an emergency, please contact: _____

Relationship: _____

Telephone: (Home) _____

(Work) _____

Relationship: _____

Telephone: (Home) _____

(Work) _____

Doctor's telephone: _____

GENERAL SCHOOL STAFF

Listed below, for your convenience, is the entire staff for the school year _____.
Please communicate directly with the staff members who can help you to help your child.

_____ School

_____ School Address

_____

_____ School Telephone

Classroom Teacher(s): _____

_____

_____

_____

_____

_____

Nurse(s): _____

_____

Librarian(s): _____

_____

Art Teacher(s): _____

_____

_____

Vocal Music Teacher(s): _____

_____

_____

Instrumental/Music Teacher(s): _____

_____

_____

Principal: _____

Vice-Principal: _____

Guidance Counselors: _____

_____

_____

_____

_____

_____

Psychologist: _____

_____

Learning Disabilities Specialist: _____

_____

Social Worker: _____

_____

Secretary(ies): _____

_____

_____

Physical Education Teacher(s): _____

_____

_____

_____

_____

_____

Basic Skills Improvement Teacher(s): ____

_____

_____

_____

Teacher(s) of the In-School Gifted: _____

_____

_____

Speech Teacher(s): _____

_____

_____

Special Education Teacher(s): _____

_____

_____

_____

Instructional Aide(s): _____

_____

_____

Other: _____

_____

_____

Custodian(s): _____

_____

_____

_____

_____

Lunch Aide(s): _____

_____

_____

_____

_____

Library Aide(s): _____

_____

_____

PTA Officers: _____

_____

_____

_____

_____

Bus Driver(s): _____

_____

_____

CLASSROOM SCHOOL STAFF

The student's classroom is the focal point of his/her education. Listed below are the staff members your child sees most often and with whom you may wish to communicate during the school year 19_____—19_____.

Classroom Teacher: _____

Art Teacher: _____

Vocal Music Teacher: _____

Instrumental Music Teacher: _____

Physical Education Teacher: _____

Librarian: _____

Nurse: _____

Other: _____

_____

_____

School Secretary: _____

Custodian: _____

Principal: _____

School Telephone: _____

School Address: _____

_____

_____

Date _____

Dear _____ ,

All the students in _____'s class are currently being tested so that their books and other materials will correspond with their present instructional level. This is an important part of the educational process in order that we may best meet the needs of each student.

Materials will be assigned when the children's groups have been determined.

Please note on your calendar the date and time of Back-to-School Night: _____. At that time you will be made aware of the studies and expectations to be stressed in this class and grade throughout the year.

Looking forward to meeting you then, I remain

Sincerely yours,

_____

Date _____

Dear _____,

    You are cordially invited to Back-to-School Night on _____
_____ at _____. It is important that you attend in order to learn about _____'s activities for the coming year.

    Please let me know by _____ whether you will attend. I have attached a schedule of the evening's events.

Sincerely,

_____

- -

_____ I (We) will attend.

_____ I am (We are) unable to attend, but please send me (us) the Back-to-School Brochure.

_____
Parent's Signature

Welcome to Back-to-School Night! Please use this form to take notes during my presentation. Thank you for attending.

_____

                                Teacher

NOTES:

_____

_____

_____

_____

_____

_____

_____

_____

_____

_____

_____

_____

_____

_____

_____

_____

_____

_____

The classroom environment must be maintained in such a way that the teacher can teach as effectively as possible and the children can learn as much as possible. Above all, consistency on my part is absolutely necessary if standards of behavior and academic progress are to be maintained and if children are to feel comfortable and happy here.

Organization is very important. The children know that upon entering the room they are to follow the directions on the board for the time between the first bell and beginning of opening exercises. Class jobs posted on the bulletin board help to keep our room and materials in working condition. These jobs rotate monthly. Some of our class rules which are also posted for all to see help to avoid the confusion which could otherwise result in a discipline problem.

Standards of behavior are essential if we are all to work and play cooperatively. Consideration for each other is stressed in our class rules and in our actions.

Every day the children spend part of the time working in small groups and as a class. There is some direct teaching and some written work. Within this structure they are given many choices as individuals. Both quiet, serious activities, and the freedom to converse, socialize and move physically are a part of every day.

1. Remember, though I try to do the right thing, I am human just like you. If you are disturbed by something or have a question, please send me a note or ask for a conference. Whatever the problem, let's talk about it. I'm sure we can work it out.

2. Read *Classroom Rules for Parents* very carefully. Your child will probably make more progress with your help.

3. See that your son or daughter gets a nutritious breakfast and enough rest.

4. Make sure that sneakers, jogging shoes, or tennis shoes are provided for gym classes on _____.

5. Check the approximate reading levels of the library books your child brings home. If the books look much too easy or much too hard, send them back.

6. Remember to provide written excuses for tardiness, as well as absences and the lunch program.

7. Try not to take your son or daughter out of school unnecessarily. Only limited homework can be provided since my plans and assignments are made almost daily to ensure that lessons are relevant to the needs of the student. Removing children from school can disturb the equilibrium of some and inadvertently imply that school isn't important to others. For those who are affected, adjustment is usually not smooth upon return to school, especially if the absence exceeds a few days.

8. Reinforce at home the rules we follow in school which relate to consideration for others. Key words such as "hello," "good-bye," "please," "thank you," "you're welcome," and "excuse me," all mean a lot.

Hints for Growing

Show Genuine Interest in Your Child's Education
–Know what's going on in the classroom.
–Listen to what happens in school.
–Go over school papers and homework.
–Talk about experiences, friends,
  assignments, etc.

Get Involved, Give Support
–Reward accomplishments.
–Work together.
–Value effort.

Limit TV Viewing

Keep Child Healthy
–Rest
–Nutritious meals
–Family meals
–Brush teeth
–Clean clothes

Encourage Good Attendance
–Get to school on time.
–Keep home when ill

Provide Study Area
–Well-lit, quiet spot
–Provide dictionary and other
  reference books.

Ideas For Learning All Year Long

Reading and Writing
–Stimulate interest in reading.
–Supply reading material.
–Encourage writing.
–Use library.
–Special events (plays, ballets)

Mathematics
–Play number games (Bingo).
–Cook together.
–Give an allowance.
–Figure things out together.
–Shop together.
–Teach how to budget.

Social Studies
–Current events (nightly news)
–Geography (globes, maps, etc.)
–Good citizen (voting)
–Observe holidays.
–Visit local govt. bldgs. and museums.

Science
–Discuss everything & anything.
–Observe plants and animals.
–Encourage collecting.
–Visit local zoo, aquarium, etc.

Create a Learning Environment

Conversation Is Important to Your Child

–Always use full sentences.

–Be attentive.

–Allow the child to express feelings to you.

–Put yourself in your child's place.

Provide a Creative Environment

–Select educational and safe toys at the child's level.

–Sing songs together.

–Share household activities and responsibilities.

–Play vocabulary building games and number games.

–Take trips to local sites.

–Allow the child to be imaginative and experimental.

Be Positive

–Have realistic expectations for your child.

–Be consistent.

–Explain limitations set.

–Encourage all efforts.

–Encourage learning from mistakes, yours and your child's.

–Your child is an individual; avoid comparisons.

Encourage Reading

–Read yourself.

–Read to your child.

–Ask questions about the story.

–Allow the child to ask questions and anticipate the ending.

–Ask your child to make up stories and tell them or read them to you.

–Make up stories with your child.

Be Involved at Home and at School

–No special training needed.

–Love, patience, interest required.

–Attend PTA meetings, school board meetings and assembly programs.

–Volunteer for library, trips, programs, etc.

1. Take your children to the public library regularly. Let them have their own cards. Guide them to the right book section but let them select their own books.

2. Check books brought home from the school library to make sure they are neither too easy nor too difficult for the child to read.

3. Set aside a time at home when everyone in the family reads for a minimum of 15 minutes each evening. As adults you set the example.

4. Listen to your child read orally and occasionally ask questions about the story or questions which will allow your child to imagine what might happen.

5. Read to your child. Set aside a special time for story telling.

6. Encourage your child to write and then read what he/she has written.

7. Develop and organize shopping lists with your child—categorize.

8. To encourage growth in vocabulary, develop lists of words of things your child sees at home, while walking, on trips, or while visiting.

9. Go for a listening walk with your child. Talk about and then list all the sounds heard.

10. Encourage your child to listen to the weather report in the morning or evening and report to the family.

11. Have your child read the ads in the newspapers and make a list of the best bargains available for your shopping list (e.g. food, appliances, cleaning products, etc.).

Date _____

Dear _____,

      An effective learning environment is achieved when students cooperatively develop, understand and abide by rules pertaining to schoolwork, homework and behavior.

      The school and home must work together. Your support is vital to your child's success. The classroom rules are listed below. Please review them

with _____.

Sincerely yours,

_____

CLASSROOM RULES ON SCHOOLWORK

1. _____
2. _____
3. _____
4. _____

CLASSROOM RULES ON HOMEWORK

1. _____
2. _____
3. _____
4. _____

CLASSROOM RULES ON BEHAVIOR

1. _____
2. _____
3. _____
4. _____

1. I will find a good way to carry materials to and from school.

2. I will take home all notes and notices.

3. I will return the notices which need to be signed on time.

4. I will give my teacher written excuses from home.

5. I will take to school _____
   or other materials on the days they are needed.

6. I will understand my homework assignments before leaving school.

7. I will set aside enough time in a quiet place to do my homework.

8. I will take finished homework to school on time.

SIGNED BY ME: _____

MY TEACHER: _____

MY MOM OR DAD: _____

1. I will listen to my teachers and my parents as they help me to plan and organize my time.

2. I will hang our weekly schedule in a place at home where I can always find it.

3. I will use the weekly schedule to remind me when assignments are due.

4. I will listen especially well to reading, math and spelling assignments because my whole group depends upon me to have them done when the group meets.

5. I will find a good way to remember on what days I need to take things to school.

6. If I miss a lesson in school because of an extra activity, I will ask a trustworthy person what I missed and do what is necessary to catch up.

7. If I miss assignments because I am absent I know that my Assignment Partner, _____, has written them down for me. _____ is the person who can deliver work to my house when I'm sick.

8. I understand that after _____ (Date) I may not call home for forgotten materials except in an emergency (such as my musical instrument on the day of the performance).

9. If my reading, math and spelling assignments are not complete and in school by the time my group meets, I will accept appropriate consequences. I understand that this is necessary to help me learn to be responsible for myself.

SIGNED BY ME: _____

MY TEACHER: _____

MY MOM OR DAD: _____

Date _____

Dear _____,
          Parent's Name

     The school provides a variety of services to assist and enhance your child's educational development. Listed below for your convenience are the special programs and activities in which _____
                                                                                    Student's Name
participates.

Program and/or Activity	**Days and Hours**
_____	_____
_____	_____
_____	_____
_____	_____
_____	_____
_____	_____

Sincerely,

_____
Teacher's Name

AFTER-SCHOOL NOTICE IIIA–16

Date: _____

Dear _____,
            Parent's Name

_____ needs to remain after school on
            Student's Name

_____, from _____ to _____ to:
            Day and Date   Time   Time

_____ Get assistance in _____.

_____ Complete unfinished classroom assignment/s _____

_____.

_____ Complete unfinished homework assignment/s _____

_____.

_____ Reflect on poor behavior.

_____ Assist _____ with _____.

_____ Attend _____.

Thank you for your cooperation,

_____
            Teacher's Signature

- -

Date: _____

Dear _____,
            Teacher's Name

_____
            Student's Name

_____ Can remain after school on _____

_____ Cannot remain after school on _____

_____ I will pick him/her up at _____ (Time)

_____ He/she may walk home at _____ (Time)

_____
            Parent's Signature

PLEASE RETURN BOTTOM PORTION

© 1989 by Parker Publishing Company

175

ABSENTEE'S HOMEWORK SHEET

Date: _____

Student's Name: _____

Phone Number: _____

Homework Partner's Name: _____

Phone Number: _____

Name of person to take assignment(s) home: _____

Phone Number: _____

Assignments

Reading: _____

Handwriting: _____

Spelling: _____

English: _____

Math: _____

Social Studies: _____

Science: _____

Current Events: _____

Creative Writing: _____

Other: _____

Books Needed

Reading: _____   Spelling: _____

Math: _____   Science: _____

Social Studies: _____   Other: _____

Teacher(s): _____

_____

Parent's Signature: _____

Date: _____

PARENTS PLEASE SIGN AND RETURN

_____ has homework in _____

_____ because he/she:

_____ was absent when we completed this work.

_____ was kept busy with extra help to supplement our work.

_____ wasn't given enough time due to an interrupted schedule.

_____ works slowly but steadily.

_____ is having difficulty with this skill.

_____ didn't follow directions.

_____ wasted time by _____.

_____ is being asked to copy a messy assignment.

- -

COMMENTS

_____

_____

_____

_____
TEACHER'S SIGNATURE

COMMENTS

_____

_____

_____

_____

_____
PARENT'S SIGNATURE

INDIVIDUALIZED ASSIGNMENT SHEET (B)

Date: _____

_____ has no homework tonight.
Student's Name

_____ has homework tonight in the following subject(s).
Student's Name

Subject: _____

Assignment: _____

_____

_____

_____

Subject: _____

Assignment: _____

_____

_____

_____

Subject: _____

Assignment: _____

_____

_____

_____

_____   _____
Teacher's Signature   Parent's Signature

Comments: _____

_____

_____

_____

_____

PLEASE RETURN THIS PAPER!

NAME: _____ DATE: _____

Subject: _____

Assignment: _____

_____

Time Worked in School: _____ Time Worked at Home: _____

Subject: _____

Assignment: _____

_____

Time Worked in School: _____ Time Worked at Home: _____

Subject: _____

Assignment: _____

_____

Time Worked in School: _____ Time Worked at Home: _____

Subject: _____

Assignment: _____

_____

Time Worked in School: _____ Time Worked at Home: _____

Questions for Parents	Yes	Needs to improve
Did he/she understand the assignments?	_____	_____
Did he/she spend too much or too little time with homework?	_____	_____
Did he/she organize his/her time at home?	_____	_____
Did he/she proofread completed work?	_____	_____
Did he/she work steadily and carefully?	_____	_____
Did he/she need your help?	_____	_____

Comments: _____

_____

_____

_____

_____
Parent's Signature

PLEASE RETURN THIS PAPER!

WEEKLY ASSIGNMENT SHEET

STUDENT'S NAME: _____

HOMEWORK FOR WEEK OF: _____

Special Assignments

Subject: _____ Date Due: _____

Assignment: _____

_____

Subject: _____ Date Due: _____

Assignment: _____

_____

Subject: _____ Date Due: _____

Assignment: _____

_____

Regular Assignments

	Subject	*Date Due*
A.	_____	
B.	_____	
C.	_____	
D.	_____	
E.	_____	
F.	_____	
G.	_____	

_____
Parent's Signature

Date: _____

To: _____

From: _____

Re: _____

The assignments listed below have been explained in detail to _____
_____. Please encourage him/her to work on all of them throughout the month. Each assignment will be accepted at school as it is completed. All are due by _____.

1. _____

2. _____

3. _____

4. _____

Parent's Signature: _____ Date: _____

PLEASE RETURN THIS PAPER WITH YOUR SIGNATURE

LONG-RANGE ASSIGNMENT

NAME: _____ DATE: _____

GRADE: _____ ROOM: _____

Name of Assignment (Project, Report, etc.) _____

Subject(s) or Unit _____

Directions: Write each part of the assignment below and the date it is due. Return the bottom portion of this paper with your parent's signature. Keep the top part in a safe place.

Assignments	Date Due
Part I	
Part II	
Part III	
Part IV	
Part V	
Part VI	

- -

Date: _____

Dear _____,
         (Teacher's Name)

    I have seen _____'s assignments and will encourage him/her to be prepared with each assignment when due.

_____
(Parent's Signature)

TO: ALL _____ GRADE STUDENTS

RE: _____

TIME: EVERY _____ OF THE MONTH FROM _____ TO

_____ BEGINNING _____. MEETING PLACE WILL BE

_____.

_____GRADE STUDENTS INTERESTED IN FOLLOWING THE

CRITERIA ON THE BULLETIN BOARD OUTSIDE THE _____

ARE INVITED TO _____.

IF YOU ARE INTERESTED PLEASE SIGN THIS SHEET AND HAVE YOUR
PARENTS SIGN, ALSO.

_____   _____
STUDENT'S SIGNATURE   PARENT'S SIGNATURE

DATE: _____

APPROVED BY: _____
          PRINCIPAL

NAME: _____ DUE DATE: _____

1. Several days before it is due have a grown-up in your family help you choose an interesting article that you can understand. Read it aloud together.

2. Choose nothing about fire, accident, death or any other violent act unless it happens to a famous person.

3. Fill in the information on the form below.

4. On the back of this paper write two interesting facts in addition to the answers below. Use sentences when you write them.

5. Practice saying the facts aloud from memory several times.

6. Bring to school the whole article and this paper on the day they are due. Give them to your teacher. Stand in front of the class and explain the article from memory loudly and clearly.

Parent's Signature: _____

- -

Who? _____

What? _____

_____

When? _____

Where? _____

How? *or* Why? _____

_____

_____

_____

NAME _____

DATE _____ GRADE _____ ROOM _____

MY NEXT PRESENTATION WILL TAKE PLACE ON _____

NAME OF NEWSPAPER OR MAGAZINE _____

DATE OF NEWSPAPER OR MAGAZINE _____

TITLE OF ARTICLE _____

ABOUT WHOM IS THE ARTICLE? _____

WHAT IS THE MOST IMPORTANT THING THAT HAPPENED? _____

_____

_____

_____

WHEN DID IT HAPPEN? _____

WHERE DID IT HAPPEN? _____

HOW OR WHY DID IT HAPPEN? _____

_____

WRITE ANOTHER INTERESTING FACT _____

_____

_____

_____

WRITE STILL ANOTHER INTERESTING FACT _____

_____

_____

_____

Parents who helped with the selection and/or presentation of the current event please sign below.

_____
Parent's Signature

PRACTICE NOTIFICATION

Date: _____

Dear _____,
       Parent's Name

_____ needs additional practice with:
       Student's Name

_____

_____

The reason for this need is:

_____

_____

_____

_____

Please help.

Thank you,

_____
       Teacher's Name

Date: _____

Dear _____,

     We are currently preparing for Parent-Teacher Conferences and will soon be sending you all the pertinent information and slips. The conference gives you the opportunity to ask questions and to talk with me/us about how your child is doing in school.

     It would be helpful if you prepared in advance for our meeting by following these suggestions:

     1. Write down anything you wish to relate to the teacher concerning your child. This will surely help the teacher better understand him/her.

     2. Write down questions you wish to ask of the teacher.

     3. Make prior appointments with other school specialists who work with your child. This will allow you to speak with them while at school.

     4. Ask your child if there is anything he/she would like you to discuss with the teacher.

     5. Please be prompt so that each parent has his/her fair share of conference time.

     6. Listen carefully to recommendations.

     7. Discuss with the teacher ways that you can assist your child in overcoming weak areas as well as capitalizing on known strengths.

     8. Don't be hesitant to discuss your concerns with your child's teacher.

Let's look forward to a productive meeting.

Sincerely yours,

_____

_____
Teacher(s) Signature(s)

In accordance with the yearly school calendar, Parent-Teacher conferences are now being planned. Before your conference can be arranged, please look at the list of available dates and times, indicating below which ones are convenient for you.

Dates: _____   Time: _____

_____   _____

_____   _____

_____   _____

_____
Teacher's Signature

Comments: _____

_____

_____

_____

_____

_____

_____

_____
Parent's Signature

A Parent-Teacher conference has been arranged with:

_____

(Parents)

and

_____

(Teacher)

at _____

(Time)

on _____

(Date)

_____

(Teacher's Signature)

Please return the form below.

- -

Date _____

Dear _____,

(Teacher's Name)

_____ I am able to attend the conference at the appointed time.

_____ I am unable to attend the conference at the appointed time.

I would particularly like to discuss the following items at the conference:

_____

_____

_____

_____

(Parent's Signature)

Date _____

Dear _____,

     Your conference appointment has been changed to accommodate your schedule. Your new appointment is for:

_____
Day

_____
Date

_____
Time

_____
Place

_____
Teacher's Signature

Please keep this top portion as a reminder.

- -

Date _____

Dear _____,

_____ I will attend the conference at the newly arranged time.

_____ I will be unable to attend.

_____
Parent's Signature

Date _____

Dear _____ Parents,
      (School)

    During this month we will be having Parent-Teacher Conferences. For most parents this conference will be optional. Please fill out the conference form below if you feel that you would like to have a conference with me. Available dates are:

_____

_____

_____

_____

Yours truly,

_____
              (Teacher)

– –

Student's Name: _____

Teacher's Name: _____

_____ I do not feel a conference is necessary at this time.

_____ A conference is requested by your child's teacher. Please indicate your choice of dates below.

_____ I would like a conference. I have indicated my choices of dates below.

Possible dates: _____

_____

Parent's Signature: _____

Date _____

Dear _____,
    (Parent)

_____ borrowed _____
    (Student)   (Material)

_____ from the school on _____
                                   (Date)

Please encourage him/her to return these item(s) no later than

_____.
    (Day)

Thank you,

_____
(Teacher's Signature)

_____
(Parent's Signature)

Date _____

Dear _____,
         (Parent)

_____ borrowed
                    (Student)

_____
                    (Material)

on _____.
        (Date)

This material is overdue and needed in the classroom. Please help him/her find these items and ensure that they are returned as soon as possible.

Thank you for your cooperation.

_____
                    (Teacher)

_____
                    (Parent)

Date _____

Dear _____,
          (Parent)

I am sorry to inform you that _____
                              (Student)

owes the following material to _____
                               (School)

Title(s) _____
              (Materials)

On _____ occasions(s) _____ reminder(s) were
      (Number)   (Number)

sent to you. Please help _____ search for the
                              (Student)

above item(s).

If not returned quickly, the replacement cost to you will be

$_____.

Sincerely yours,

_____
          (Teacher)

Please sign below and return this notice.

_____
       (Parent's Signature)

Date _____

Dear Parent,

    This is to inform you that _____ has just

completed a unit in _____

_____.

We are now beginning a study of _____

_____

and would appreciate your assistance with _____

_____.

Sincerely yours,

_____
(Teacher)

Date _____

Dear Parent,

Our class is busily preparing for an assembly program about

_____,

to be presented on _____.

Please note the date on your calendar so that you can attend. Further information will be forthcoming.

Sincerely yours,

_____
(Teacher)

- -

Date _____

Dear Parent,

Our class is busily preparing for an assembly program about

_____,

to be presented on _____.

Please note the date on your calendar so that you can attend. Further information will be forthcoming.

Sincerely yours,

_____
(Teacher)

Date _____

Dear _____,

_____'s class is excited about our up-coming trip
to _____ in connection with our
study(ies) of _____
_____.

The purpose of our visit is to expand the educational
experiences of our students. We would appreciate your
cooperation in preparing _____ for this trip by
stressing appropriate behavior, proper attire, and a positive
attitude toward the learning experience.

When you receive the *Field Trip Permission Slip,* please fill in
the required information, sign it, and return it promptly.
Additionally, please include full payment for all fees.

If there are any problems, please advise us so that we can
help. We wish all children to participate.

Sincerely yours,

_____
(Teacher)

Date _____

Dear _____,

    You are cordially invited to join _____'s class on
_____ at _____ when I will demonstrate
_____
which has already been assigned. The entire project is due on
_____.

    Your presence at the demonstration is not required since
written directions have already been distributed. Additional
copies will be available on _____.

    We look forward to seeing you, if possible.

               Yours truly,

_____

(Teacher)

You are cordially invited
to attend

_____

on

_____

at

_____

place

_____

RSVP by _____

- -

INVITATION

You are cordially invited
to attend

_____

on

_____

at

_____

place

_____

RSVP by _____

The Seth Boyden Staff and Students
request the pleasure of your
company
at a
Special Ceremony
dedicating
The Doris Froehlich Outdoor Education Center
on
Wednesday, March 27, 1989
2:30 P.M.

274 Boyden Avenue
Maplewood, New Jersey

R.S.V.P.
by March 25th
762-5600

- -

INVITATION (A): SPECIAL EVENT SAMPLE

The Seth Boyden Staff and Students
request the pleasure of your
company
at a
Special Ceremony
dedicating
The Doris Froehlich Outdoor Education Center
on
Wednesday, March 27, 1989
2:30 P.M.

274 Boyden Avenue
Maplewood, New Jersey

R.S.V.P.
by March 25th
762-5600

Your are cordially invited
to attend a
"Greek Festival"
on
Monday, March 25, 1989
at
10:15 A.M.
Jefferson School Auditorium
followed by a Luncheon

R.S.V.P.
by March 20, 1989

INVITATION (B): SPECIAL EVENT SAMPLE

Your are cordially invited
to attend a
"Greek Festival"
on
Monday, March 25, 1989
at
10:15 A.M.
Jefferson School Auditorium
followed by a Luncheon

R.S.V.P.
by March 20, 1989

Reporting
to
Parents

INFORMATION/EXPECTATIONS SHEET FROM PARENTS

Date _____

Dear _____,

Please indicate any significant information in _____'s
background which would be helpful to his/her teachers this year
(medical, personal, school history, personality, etc.).

_____

_____

_____

_____

_____

_____

Please identify your expectations for him/her this year in school.

_____

_____

_____

_____

_____

_____

Thank you,

_____

Teacher's Signature

TO STUDENTS:

1. This card is to help you do better in the areas of "behavior," "schoolwork" and "homework."

2. Give this card to your parents.

3. Discuss the ratings with your parents and have them sign the card.

4. Bring the card back to your homeroom teacher.

5. If you have any questions about your ratings, discuss them with your teacher.

TO PARENTS:

1. This Supplementary Report Card is a tool designed to increase communication between your child, his/her teacher and you, the parent.

2. The student's successes as well as problem areas are pointed out for recognition or further help.

3. Please read the card. Discussion should be positive and constructive; aimed at helping your child find ways to improve.

4. Please sign and return the card with your child.

- -

Name _____   Date _____

Ratings listed below indicate: 1 = Poor; 2 = Fair; 3 = Good; 4 = Excellent

Behavior: **1 2 3 4**   Schoolwork: **1 2 3 4**   Homework: **1 2 3 4**

Reasons for ratings marked 1 or 2 are: _____

_____

_____

_____

_____

_____   _____
Teacher's Signature   Teacher's Signature

_____
Parent's Signature

Next report will be sent on: _____
Date

IIIB-3 EVALUATION FORM FOR FALL CONFERENECE

NAME: _____   DATE: _____

TEACHERS: GRADE: _____

_____

_____

_____

Language Arts/Reading: _____
_____

Language Arts/ English: _____
_____

Language Arts/Spelling: _____
_____

Language Arts/Handwriting: _____
_____

Language Arts/Creative Writing: _____
_____

Mathematics: _____
_____

Science: _____
_____

Social Studies: _____
_____

- -

Uses time to good advantage _____   Listens attentively _____
Completes assigned work _____   Is dependable _____
Participates in discussions _____   Follows directions _____
Observes school and class rules _____   Practices self-control _____
Is self-motivated _____   Is well organized _____
Has a cooperative attitude _____   Works independently _____

Date _____

Dear _____,
  (Parent or Guardian)

Below is an assessment of _____'s work in each of the subjects I teach him/her. Please review them closely and feel free to contact me if you have any questions. Your comments in the space provided below would be appreciated. Please sign and return this report.

Sincerely yours,

_____
  (Special Teacher)

Subject: _____
_____
_____
_____

Subject: _____
_____
_____
_____

Parent/Guardian's Comments _____
_____
_____
_____

_____
  (Parent/Guardian Signature)

POSITIVE PROGRESS REPORT

Dear _____,

    You can be proud, your child _____ has earned
this special note for _____

_____

_____

_____

_____

_____

_____

Signed: _____   Date _____
           (Teacher)

- -

POSITIVE PROGRESS REPORT

Dear _____,

    You can be proud, your child _____ has earned
this special note for _____

_____

_____

_____

_____

_____

_____

Signed: _____   Date _____
           (Teacher)

Date _____

Dear _____ ,

Today, _____ 's behavior was _____

_____

_____

_____ .

It would be helpful if you _____

_____ .

Thank you, _____
(Teacher)

- -

BEHAVIOR REPORT

Date _____

Dear _____ ,

Today, _____ 's behavior was _____

_____

_____

_____ .

It would be helpful if you _____

_____ .

Thank you, _____
(Teacher)

IIIB–7 EVALUATION FORM FOR SPRING CONFERENCE

NAME: _____   CONFERENCE DATE: _____

Good achievement/progress has been made this year in the following areas:

Academic	Work Habits/Study Skills	Personal Development

Areas needing improvement are:

Academic	Work Habits/Study Skills	Personal Development

Parents
as
Resources

_____

Date

Dear _____,

Thank you for volunteering to be the classroom parent for
_____. During the year I will
ask for your assistance in organizing enrichment activities for our class and
coordinating parent volunteers to help with these activities.

I appreciate your interest and cooperation and look forward to
working with you this year in order to provide rewarding, supplementary
educational experiences for our students.

Sincerely yours,

_____

Teacher

NAME: _____ TELEPHONE: _____

ADDRESS: _____

Your time and talents are needed to enhance and enrich this year's educational program in _____ class. Please complete and return this survey in the spirit of mutual enjoyment and cooperation.

1. My educational background: (optional) _____

2. My job: _____

3. My hobby(ies): _____

4. I am willing to speak to the class about _____

5. I can demonstrate _____

6. I know someone who can speak about/demonstrate _____
   _____

7. I am willing to assist the teacher during school time in the following areas: (Please check)

   _____ a) assisting children with assignments

   _____ b) marking papers

   _____ c) putting up bulletin boards

   _____ d) field trip chaperon

   _____ e) special projects (art, science experiments, etc.)

   _____ f) assembly preparation/production

   _____ g) _____

   _____ h) _____

8. I can arrange a class trip to _____

9. I can transport children in my car on field trips. _____
   Yes or No

10. I am willing to help with assembly preparation/production in the following ways: (Please check)

    a) scenery _____   f) prompting _____

    b) costumes _____   g) piano accompaniment _____

    c) props _____   h) dance steps _____

    d) makeup _____   i) _____ _____

    e) programs _____   j) _____ _____

11. I am willing to cook or bake for multicultural events, parties or picnics. _____
    Yes or No

REQUEST FOR PARENTAL ASSISTANCE

_____
(Date)

Dear _____:

Your assistance is needed for:

    Event: _____

    Date: _____

    Time: _____

    Place: _____

    Transportation (if needed): _____

    Please bring (if needed): _____

                       Thanks for your help!

                   Signed: _____
                              Teacher's Signature

- -

Please check one and return.

☐   I will be able to assist

    on _____
                   day, date, time

    for _____
                     event

☐   At this time I am unable to assist

    on _____
                   day, date, time

    for _____
                     event

                     _____
                              Parent's Signature

Name of Parent	Telephone # Home/Work	Activity

IIIC–5 GROUP LEADER FIELD TRIP INSTRUCTION SHEET

TRIP: _____

LEADER: (PARENT) _____

STUDENTS IN GROUP: _____

_____

_____

_____

_____

_____

ASSIGNMENT:

      TIME OF ARRIVAL AT SCHOOL: _____

      TIME OF DEPARTURE FROM SCHOOL: _____

      TIME OF DEPARTURE FROM TRIP SITE: _____

      TIME OF ARRIVAL AT SCHOOL (APPROXIMATE): _____

      KEEP YOUR GROUP TOGETHER WHEN WE ARRIVE AT _____

      _____.

      PLEASE REMAIN WITH YOUR GROUP THROUGHOUT THE TRIP. IF YOU NEED TO LEAVE THE GROUP PLEASE ADVISE THE TEACHER.

      THE TEACHER EXPECTS YOUR SUPPORT IN MAINTAINING ORDER.

      THANK YOU FOR VOLUNTEERING YOUR SERVICES. WE ARE MOST APPRECIATIVE OF YOUR INTEREST. HAVE A GOOD DAY.

GROUP I: _____ WILL ATTEND _____

FROM _____ TO _____.

GROUP II: _____ WILL ATTEND _____

FROM _____ TO _____.

AT _____ GROUP I WILL ATTEND _____

AND GROUP II WILL ATTEND _____.

AT _____ ALL GROUPS WILL PICK UP LUNCHES AND PROCEED TO DESIGNATED AREA FOR LUNCH. AFTER EATING MAKE SURE TO CLEAN UP.

FROM _____ TO _____ STUDENTS MAY GO TO BATHROOM, BUY SOUVENIERS

AND VISIT _____.

AT _____ GROUP I WILL ATTEND _____

_____ AND GROUP II WILL ATTEND _____

_____.

AT _____ GROUP I WILL ATTEND _____

AND GROUP II WILL ATTEND _____.

AT _____ ALL GROUPS ARE TO MEET _____

FOR DEPARTURE TO SCHOOL.

THE BRONX ZOO

GROUP LEADER: _____

STUDENTS IN GROUP: _____

_____

This packet contains instructions, a zoo map and two worksheets.

INSTRUCTIONS

1. The group remains together during the entire trip: bus, zoo, lunch, zoo, bus.

2. Groups may go in any direction separately or two together as long as the following areas are visited:

   A. House of Darkness

   B. World of Birds

   C. World of Reptiles

   D. Small Mammals

3. Note on your map the refreshment stands, rest room facilities, first-aid and lost-and-found (including children) stations.

4. Stop for *LUNCH* at any refreshment stand between 11:30 and 11:45. Give yourselves 30 to 40 minutes for lunch. Clean up the area before leaving.

5. Meet at the *Starting Gate* at 1:30. We must leave the Bronx Zoo together not later than 1:35.

THANK YOU FOR VOLUNTEERING AND FOR YOUR TREMENDOUS HELP.

HAVE A GOOD TIME!

GROUP LEADER: _____

GROUP: _____

BRONX ZOO WORKSHEETS

INSTRUCTIONS: The group leader should write down the information suggested by
the group after visiting each area of the zoo.

I. List ten mammals you observed and their habitats.

Mammal	*Habitat*
_____	_____
_____	_____
_____	_____
_____	_____
_____	_____
_____	_____
_____	_____
_____	_____
_____	_____
_____	_____

II. List five reptiles you saw and their habitats.

Reptile	*Habitat*
_____	_____
_____	_____
_____	_____
_____	_____
_____	_____

III. What animals did you see in the House of Darkness?

_____

_____

_____

_____

IV. List ten birds you observed and their habitats.

<table>
<tr><td>Bird</td><td>Habitat</td></tr>
</table>

Bird	Habitat
_____	_____
_____	_____
_____	_____
_____	_____
_____	_____
_____	_____
_____	_____
_____	_____

V. What else of interest did you see?

_____

_____

_____

_____

_____

_____

VI. What did you find to be the most fascinating animal? Tell why. If your group cannot agree on one, list all your choices.

_____

_____

_____

_____

_____

_____

Section IV

FORMS FOR PROFESSIONAL GROWTH AND DEVELOPMENT

Continuous education is desirable for the improvement of professional skills and techniques. Periodic self-evaluation provides the needed impetus to affirm or change current practices. From new learning comes growth which, in turn, ensures a better teaching environment for students, an informed source for colleagues, respect for self, and the enhancement of the teaching profession as a whole.

EXPLANATORY NOTES

Form IV–7: See note for Form IV–8.

Form IV–8: Questions are identical on both the "Student Teacher Evaluation" and the "Self-Evaluation for Student Teacher." Use both forms to compare your perceptions. Communication is the key.

Form IV–10: We chose this form to be the final one in this book. If you answered "yes" to each of the 20 questions, we'd like to think it's because you found forms to assist you in each mentioned category!

Forms for Professional Growth and Development

COURSE/WORKSHOP/INSERVICE RECORD

NAME: _____

Course Title			
Dates Taken	Place		Number of Credits
Cost Per Credit	Total Cost	Date Transcript Requested	Transcript Received by Administration

NAME: _____

Course Title			
Dates Taken	Place		Number of Credits
Cost Per Credit	Total Cost	Date Transcript Requested	Transcript Received by Administration

NAME: _____

Course Title			
Dates Taken	Place		Number of Credits
Cost Per Credit	Total Cost	Date Transcript Requested	Transcript Received by Administration

NAME: _____

Course Title			
Dates Taken	Place		Number of Credits
Cost Per Credit	Total Cost	Date Transcript Requested	Transcript Received by Administration

Name of Convention:	Place:		Dates:
Transportation: (Type)	Transportation Expenses:	Meal Expenses:	
Hotel/Motel Expenses:	# of Days Attending:	Miscellaneous Professional Expenses:	Total Cost:

Workspace is provided below to help you tally total expenses.

First Day:

Second Day:

Third Day:

Fourth Day:

PROFESSIONAL LIBRARY EXPENSE RECORD		
Title of Book, Magazine, Cassette, etc.	Cost	Date

PROFESSIONAL ORGANIZATION DUES RECORD			
Name of Organization	Date of Initial Membership	Date of Renewal	Cost

NAME: _____

Date(s)	To:	By Means of:	Reason	Total Cost
	From:	By Means of:		

Date(s)	To:	By Means of:	Reason	Total Cost
	From:	By Means of:		

Date(s)	To:	By Means of:	Reason	Total Cost
	From:	By Means of:		

Date(s)	To:	By Means of:	Reason	Total Cost
	From:	By Means of:		

Date(s)	To:	By Means of:	Reason	Total Cost
	From:	By Means of:		

Date(s)	To:	By Means of:	Reason	Total Cost
	From:	By Means of:		

LOSS-OF-PREPARATION-TIME FORM

NAME: _____

SCHOOL: _____ POSITION: _____

DATE	TIMES	TOTAL TIME	REASON	COMPEN- SATION

Name: _____   Telephone Number: _____

Address: _____

What are you applying for?

OBJECTIVE:

What jobs have you held which qualify you for your objective, beginning with your present position (ex. 1985–1987, 1982–1985 and so forth)? Then write and underline your title first, location second. Describe your responsibilities using sentences or phrases. Be consistent.

EXPERIENCE:

19_____–19_____   Title, Location (Underlined)

Responsibilities:

19_____–19_____   Title, Location (Underlined)

Responsibilities:

RESUMÉ PLANNING

What professional committees have you chaired, served on? What professional organizations have you actively participated in? Dates are optional. Begin with present.

PROFESSIONAL ACTIVITIES:

19_____–_____

Title, Committee or Organization (Underlined)

Responsibilities:

Indicate any experience outside your work (a published article, active community involvement, etc.) Dates are optional.

RELATED EXPERIENCE:

Title, Location

Responsibilities or Description:

Omit this section if not applicable.

LANGUAGES:

List degree, college or university, location, (beginning with most recent). Next, list locations where additional courses and/or inservices were taken. Dates are optional.

EDUCATION:

Consult other sources when finalizing your resumé.

Write a cover letter telling what position you are applying for, why you are doing so and what you can contribute to those you will be serving. Follow your interview with a thank-you letter.

MY STUDENT TEACHER: YES | NO

1. Arrives before the children and leaves after them.

2. Calls me and/or the school when ill or an emergency arises.

3. Projects a professional appearance.

4. Established and now maintains a professional relationship with children.

5. Is neither overbearing nor too familiar with me or other staff members.

6. Maintains self-control by restraining his/her emotions; discusses problems calmly.

7. Knows the state laws regarding corporal punishment.

8. Uses a firm but natural tone of voice when disciplining children.

9. Sets realistic standards for work and behavior and sticks to them.

10. Tries to discipline individuals separately from the group.

11. Adopts my effective classroom management techniques.

12. Uses proper English.

13. Modulates his/her voice to achieve the desired classroom mood.

14. Spells correctly; uses the dictionary when necessary.

15. Recognizes the negative but emphasizes the positive in all aspects of his/her student teaching role.

16. Asks appropriate questions.

17. Offers to assist me.

18. Works quickly and carefully.

19. Researches subject matter.

20. Creates appropriate teaching materials.

SELF-EVALUATION FOR STUDENT TEACHER

This will be used during a conference with your cooperating teacher to analyze and discuss perceived strengths and weaknesses.

YES | NO

1. I arrive before the children and leave after them.

2. I call my cooperating teacher and/or school when ill or an emergency arises.

3. I project a professional appearance.

4. I establish and maintain a professional relationship with children.

5. I am neither overbearing nor too familiar with my cooperating teacher and other staff members.

6. I maintain self-control by restraining my emotions; I discuss problems calmly.

7. I know the state laws regarding corporal punishment.

8. I use a firm but natural tone of voice when disciplining children.

9. I set realistic standards for work and behavior and stick to them.

10. I try to discipline individuals separately from the group.

11. I adopt the effective classroom management techniques of my cooperating teacher.

12. I use proper English.

13. I modulate my voice to achieve desired classroom moods.

14. I spell correctly. I use the dictionary when necessary.

15. I recognize the negative but emphasize the positive in all aspects of my role as student teacher.

16. I ask appropriate questions.

17. I offer to assist my cooperating teacher.

18. I work quickly and carefully.

19. I research subject matter.

20. I create appropriate teaching materials.

Answer "yes" to Questions A–Z below and feel a surge of pride in starting someone on the road to teaching success. We've chosen the pronoun "her" because most student teachers at the elementary level are women.

		YES	NO
A.	Did I introduce her to the staff?		
B.	Did I take her on a tour of the building?		
C.	Do I include her in schoolwide programs and activities?		
D.	Do I present her to my class as our helping or interning teacher rather than a student?		
E.	Do I confer with her when setting classroom goals?		
F.	Do I share the feelings of the students with her?		
G.	Do I effectively demonstrate my teaching skill?		
H.	Do I establish things to look for during her observation time?		
I.	Do I share available resources and instructional materials?		
J.	Do I demonstrate how to create materials when none exist?		
K.	Do I share workspace?		
L.	Do I discuss my own teaching failures as well as my successes?		
M.	Do I comment on her strengths as well as weaknesses?		
N.	Do I "sandwich" criticism between two positive comments?		
O.	Do I help her evaluate what worked, what didn't work and why?		
P.	Do I have frequent and regular conferences with her?		
Q.	Am I supportive as she prepares for a visit from her supervisor?		
R.	Do I encourage her self-confidence when appropriate?		
S.	Do I mention my displeasure when her mistakes persist?		
T.	Do I allow for her growth, development and originality?		
U.	Do I inform her of reasonable standards and expectations?		
V.	Do I acquaint her with class records, standardized test scores and pertinent procedures?		
W.	Do I inform her of ordering procedures for media?		
X.	Do I teach her how to use the media?		
Y.	Do I include her as an observer during parent-teacher conferences?		
Z.	Do I discuss with her ways to use information about the students to promote their positive growth and development?		

Answer yes or no to the questions below:

	YES	NO

1. I can find the materials I need when I want them.

2. I have a clear idea of what I must order.

3. My record keeping helps me to plan effectively.

4. The clerical aspects of my job are manageable.

5. Information which I've gathered about my students is accessible to me and my colleagues.

6. I can support my evaluation of my students.

7. I help my students understand their responsibilities in relation to schoolwork, homework and behavior.

8. I give my students clear and reasonable assignments.

9. I provide means by which my students can organize their time and materials effectively.

10. I give my students many opportunities to grow and develop.

11. My decisions are considered to be fair by my students and their parents.

12. I establish good rapport wherein students feel they can talk over problems.

13. I provide a safe, stable environment in which my students can learn.

14. I keep parents apprised of classroom work and activities.

15. I keep parents informed regarding their children's progress.

16. I provide the opportunity for parents to participate in class activities.

17. I provide opportunities for parents to discuss concerns.

18. I help parents understand how they can help their children get the most out of school.

19. I continue to improve my teaching skills:

    a. through attendance at courses, workshops, inservice training sessions, conferences and conventions.

    b. by reading educational publications.

20. Wow! I'm a terrific teacher!